eople

God's Diverse People

LAWRENCE and DIANA OSBORN

Foreword by Bishop Michael Whinney

daybreak

London

First published in 1991 by
Daybreak
Darton, Longman and Todd Ltd
89 Lillie Road, London SW6 1UD

ISBN 0–232–51878–5

A catalogue record of this book is available
from the British Library

The Scripture quotations in this publication are from the
Revised Standard Version of the Bible, copyrighted 1971 and
1952 by the Division of Christian Education of the National
Council of the Churches of Christ in the USA

Cover design by Sarah John

Phototypeset by Intype, London
Printed and bound in Great Britain
by Courier International Ltd, East Kilbride

Contents

Acknowledgement

Many people have contributed ... to this book. In particular ... for introducing us to the ... Jeanette Renouf for training ... on for making available to us Bishop Ole Hal... temperament and the Christian life. And Re... or efficient editor... work and helpful comment... drafts. We are also grateful to the many friends... ners who have acted as guinea pi... before and ... paration of this volume

Foreword

At last someone in Britain has provided us with a clear guide
to the Myers–Briggs Type Indicator (MBTI). Books from
America have not always been helpful because of difference in
idiom, but now Diana and Lawrence Osborn have overcome
this difficulty by writing from within our own understanding
and appreciation about this useful tool.

This guide to personality preferences is particularly welcome
at a time when the MBTI's use in Britain is growing so rapidly
and when the need to understand its application is vital. Its
misuse in 'screening out' some applicants from particular jobs
is highly unethical and the authors make that clear. Thankfully
they show us the positive benefits in all areas of activity of this
approach to human behaviour.

Diana and Lawrence write as committed Christians and show
us how helpful this development of Carl Jung's work on differing personality types can be to all of us in our journeying
with Christ. The later chapters on prayer, communication and
Christian leadership contain a wealth of insights and practical
suggestions culled from their wide experience. The exercises at
the end of each chapter can be done either individually or in
groups and are well worth while attempting.

The need to know your own type preferences with their
strengths and weaknesses is demonstrated clearly in the section
in Chapter 6 on Type and Pastoral Counselling. The wise warn-
ings both here and in the earlier chapter on the dangers of
stereotyping people into prayer styles should be heeded by all
in any position of leadership in the Churches. Similarly, the

cautiousness in using American statistics about types in the Churches in Chapter 5 is appropriate, for as yet not enough data has been collected in Britain to give us an accurate picture of how we may differ this side of the Atlantic.

The last chapter takes us beyond a limited and defective view of personal growth as being entirely achieved by the natural process of developing innate potential by human effort and presents the specifically Christian concept of grace. The authors stress that differences of temperament are not suppressed by the process of transformation that accompanies faith in Christ but are actually enriched.

As someone who uses the Myers–Briggs Type Indicator constantly in my work as a leader, pastor and counsellor, I am grateful to Diana and Lawrence Osborn for putting into my hands a book to which I shall refer constantly and lend frequently. While it is a particularly relevant and helpful handbook for all Christian leaders, its application is far wider than the task facing the Churches today and it will appeal to all types.

MICHAEL DICKENS· WHINNEY
Assistant Bishop
Diocese of Birmingham

1

Many Members, One Body

We live in a world of tremendous variety. Part of that variety is the tremendous range of human attitudes and behaviour. No two people ever seem to react in precisely the same way to the same situation. This can be the source of endless trouble, confusion, and division. But it can also be the basis of fresh opportunities, possibilities, and mutual enrichment.

This book has been written in the belief that many of those differences in attitude and behaviour can be traced to a few clearly defined, but nevertheless fundamental, psychological differences. Taken together these fundamental differences constitute our temperament or psychological type.

Of course temperament is only one among many factors which, taken together, predispose us to act or behave in one way rather than another. It must take its place alongside differences of race, culture, nationality, and social class (or economic status). Physiological factors such as sexuality, age, and handicap also colour our experience of the world and, hence, affect the way we respond to it and to one another. Nevertheless, in our experience, temperament is particularly significant at the level of personal and social relationships.

But what do we mean by temperament? To begin with, it should already be clear that it is only one aspect of our total personality. But it is a fundamental aspect. A simple working definition might be that temperament is our instinctive (or unconscious) tendency to respond in a particular way to our surroundings. Thus it precedes (and may be submerged under) the responses we learn as a result of all the other factors we

1

have mentioned. It is only a tendency, not a set of biological rules which somehow determines our behaviour, and it may be overridden by the exercise of our wills.

Finally, it is not to be confused with character. In itself, temperament is neither good nor bad. We cannot identify some temperaments rather than others with immoral behaviour. Nor can we say that certain temperaments result in good behaviour. What we can say is that our temperament may incline us to particular *forms* of moral or immoral behaviour.

That great Norwegian evangelical bishop, Ole Hallesby, once offered a helpful musical analogy for temperament when he said, 'It strikes the key or chord to which the soul must vibrate.'[1] Stringed instruments such as guitars or violins may be tuned in a variety of different ways. An infinite variety of tunes may be played on them but that tuning remains fundamental. Similarly the natural rhythm of our lives is set by our temperament.

But should we place such emphasis on our differences? Surely the vision set before us in the New Testament is of a community in which all temporal differences are overcome and transcended by the unity offered by Christ. After all, Paul apparently dismissed some of the other factors which divide us in the following terms: 'There is neither Jew nor Greek, there is neither slave nor free, there is neither male nor female; for you are all one in Christ Jesus' (Gal. 3:28).

PAUL'S VISION OF UNITY-IN-DIVERSITY

The passage we have just quoted is but one of many in which Paul sets before us a vision of unity in Christ Jesus. Perhaps because of the bitter divisions within the Galatian church, he places particular stress on our oneness in Christ. Elsewhere we find a more carefully nuanced account of that unity. It is clear that, whatever else he may have thought, Paul did not envisage this unity as an undifferentiated uniformity. Take, for example, his marvellous description of the Church as the body of Christ in 1 Corinthians 12:

> by one Spirit we were all baptized into one body – Jews or Greeks, slaves or free – and all were made to drink of one Spirit.
>
> For the body does not consist of one member but of many. If the foot should say, 'Because I am not a hand, I do not belong to the body,' that would not make it any less a part of the body. And if the ear should say, 'Because I am not an eye, I do not belong to the body,' that would not make it any less a part of the body. If the whole body were an eye, where would be the hearing? If the whole body were an ear, where would be the sense of smell? But as it is, God arranged the organs in the body, each one of them, as he chose. If all were a single organ, where would the body be? As it is, there are many parts, yet one body. The eye cannot say to the hand, 'I have no need of you,' nor again the head to the feet, 'I have no need of you.'   (12–21)

The apostle Paul clearly envisaged the Church as a rich diversity. It was capable of containing people of all social classes, of different races, and of both sexes. It could accommodate different educational backgrounds, different ways of life, different temperaments, and different gifts (both natural and spiritual). In fact, one could go further and suggest that the Church is actually called to reflect the full diversity of humankind within its number. This surely is implicit in John's apocalyptic vision of 'a great multitude . . . from every nation, from all tribes and peoples and tongues' (Rev. 7:9) gathered before the throne of God to offer him praise.

But above all, Paul expected the Church to unite this incredible range of human strength and weakness without destroying the richness of its diversity. The nuclear physicist, the cabinet maker, the shepherd, and the housewife are to be united in Christ by the Holy Spirit without losing or suppressing the distinctive skills, characters, and handicaps which make them unique human beings.

Far from abolishing our differences, the Church of Paul's vision *fulfils* them. The community he envisaged is one which affirms our individuality. But it does not leave us as mere individuals. No, it brings us all together and fits us, in our individuality, into the body of Christ, into the temple of God (Eph. 2:20–2). Picking up Hallesby's musical analogy, membership of the Church offers each one of us a unique part in the universal symphony of praise to God our creator and redeemer.

Paul's vision, with its celebration of individuality, contrasts sharply with the natural tendency of human societies. Generally speaking, they do not take kindly to people who are different. They may despise, marginalise, or persecute those who stand out because of colour, physical or mental disability, or convictions (whether religious, political, or philosophical). Even when such discrimination is not apparent, every human society or institution exerts a tremendous pressure to conform to its norms of behaviour, appearance and belief.

This is highlighted by certain features of our own society. In some respects it is more like a machine than a body. A recent television advertisement in praise of the Government's training programme illustrates what we mean. The advertisement begins with a hole in the ground and an enormous stone block which does not fit it. A horde of ant-like workers are unleashed upon it and the final image is of the block dropping neatly into the hole. The caption is 'Training the workers without jobs to fill the jobs without workers'. The impression it creates is of an impersonal system moulding us to fit in where it needs us. Charlie Chaplin made a similar point in the film *Modern Times*: the little man was enslaved to the mechanised production line.

That pressure towards faceless uniformity has often been cited as one of the reasons behind the emergence of the counter-culture and its successor, the New Age movement. For example, the social historian, Theodore Roszak, suggests that the root of the matter was that a generation of peculiarly sensitive young people (or pampered and spoiled kids, if you prefer) found themselves being subtly manoeuvred into careers and social roles, into tastes and values, into an all-encompassing sense of reality which had been prefabricated for them by the commanding powers of a high industrial economy. They discovered that they were being systematically processed and adapted – *used* by faceless forces, insensitive institutions which did not know who they were and did not care to know.[2]

Ironically the reaction against uniformity created its own pressure to conform. At the height of the permissive generation you just weren't 'with it' unless you embraced an irresponsible individualism. In the swinging sixties conformity meant 'doing your own thing' and refusing to conform!

Perhaps it is no coincidence that one of Paul's descriptions of our unity-in-diversity follows on immediately from his famous exhortation, 'Do not be conformed to this world but be transformed by the renewal of your mind' (Rom. 12:2). The world, unredeemed human society, appears to offer us a choice between faceless uniformity and rampant individualism. Paul envisaged a third option within the Church.

The Importance of Temperament

We believe that the effort to understand human temperament is well worth making. This is not merely a piece of theoretical psychology but an issue with important practical implications for understanding ourselves and those around us. Thus it also has important implications for our expression of the Christian faith (both public and private).

Understanding ourselves

Understanding our own temperament is about learning to recognise our own natural psychological rhythms. In a society which seems to put more pressure on its members than any previous society this has an immediate pay-off: it may help us understand and avoid certain sources of stress specific to our temperament. Conversely, it may help us to identify those possibilities which would make best use of our particular strengths.

But this recognition is not fatalistic. As we have already noted, we can override our temperament. Recognising that we tend to respond in this way rather than that is not a formula for fatalism. We need not say, 'This is how I am, I have no choice in the matter.' Rather, it is a matter of achieving a better understanding of the raw material from which our natural behaviour is constructed. Being more aware of our instinctive tendencies actually gives us greater freedom of choice: it frees us to decide whether our instinctive reaction is appropriate in this situation. Furthermore, as Christians we believe that God may graciously enable us to transcend the limitations of our natural instinctive behaviour patterns.

A better understanding of our own temperament allows us to recognise some of the potential strengths and weaknesses in our personality. As far as weaknesses are concerned, it may enable us to spot danger areas. We have already mentioned stress. Another dimension of this would be the question of the errors or sins to which we are most susceptible. We are all fallible, but different temperaments may incline us to different kinds of error. We are all sinners, but our different temperaments may lead us to express that sinfulness in different ways.[3]

In a more positive vein, an understanding of temperament may enable us to recognise and affirm possible natural gifts. This can be particularly valuable when the gifts arising from our temperament contradict the social stereotypes imposed upon people of our colour, sex, or social background. Thus, for example, women whose temperament inclines them to be logical and analytical can find affirmation within such self-understanding. This may enable them to resist the expectation that they be warm, emotional, or motherly. And, of course, the converse is true for men.

Temperament also has a significant part to play in the way we express our Christian faith. Some spiritual disciplines are more appropriate to people of one temperament than another. A knowledge of our own temperament may help us to recognise that certain models of the Christian life are simply not suitable for us. After all, whatever else is involved, living the Christian life entails being *ourselves* before God. Struggling to be a pale imitation of Hudson Taylor, or John Wesley, or St Francis of Assisi or Mother Teresa will not help us to become more mature Christians.

Understanding others

Judging another person's behaviour on the basis of our own instincts is a recipe for misunderstanding and injustice. Taking the trouble to understand something of the diversity of human temperaments (their different weaknesses and, more importantly, their potential strengths) is a firm foundation for improved personal relationships.

It is often said that we fear what we do not understand. Thus we may despise, dismiss, or dislike people whose behaviour seems alien. But if we seek an explanation of why they respond differently, our fear may give way to respect and we may find it easier to obey our Lord's command to love them.

Even when we do not consciously dislike the other person, a failure to understand that they are temperamentally different from us may lead to a breakdown in communications. We may think we are talking to that person, but in reality we are talking to ourselves; and what that person is hearing is not at all what we intended to say. It is natural enough, when asked for advice, to say what we think or feel we would need to hear in that situation.

Some understanding of temperament would help us to recall the possibility of misunderstanding. Precisely the same might be said of our preaching and evangelism. A recognition that what we say may not be what the other person hears is a first step towards more effective communication.

Obstacles to understanding temperament

In spite of the clear advantages of understanding human temperament, there is still a certain reticence to talk about and allow for psychological differences.

One possible reason for this is a degree of scepticism within our culture about the significance of such differences. The materialism which has dominated western society has tended to discourage the development of a rich and consistent vocabulary with which to discuss such matters. On the contrary, anything to do with the soul or the psyche has been regarded as somehow less real than quantifiable material phenomena. We rely upon the images created by poets and novelists; men and women who very often find themselves on the fringes of society.

Another reason specific to Christians is a suspicion of too great an interest in the self. Over the centuries some Christian traditions have transformed the biblical injunction to love your neighbour as yourself into a command to love your neighbour instead of yourself. Luther, in particular, appeared to believe that love of self precluded love of God and neighbour: that in order to love God and your neighbour, you had first to hate yourself. However, far from helping us understand one another better, such self-hatred has the effect of preventing us from achieving the kind of realistic self-understanding which can be an effective foundation for understanding and, hence, loving others.

WAYS OF DESCRIBING TEMPERAMENT

In spite of these hindrances, philosophers and scientists have from ancient times tried to make sense of the diversity of human temperaments. They have sought patterns within the apparent chaos of human behaviour.

The four temperaments

The most venerable western way of classifying these differences is the system of four temperaments devised by the ancient physician Galen. He assumed that the particular psychological functioning of each individual was determined by his or her particular mixture of bodily fluids (in fact, temperament is derived from the Latin word for a mixture). Since, in the tradition of Hippocratic medicine, there were supposed to be four bodily fluids, this gave rise to four 'ideal' temperament types: sanguine, melancholic, choleric, and phlegmatic (depending on which of the fluids was dominant).

Although the underlying physiological theory has long since been discarded, the four temperaments do seem to reflect real differences in human psychology. That generations of men and women have found this classification useful is clear from the fact that they have won for themselves a permanent place in the language.

In fact, this system is still used today to explain differences in human personality. The pioneers of experimental psychology in the nineteenth century attempted to relate the temperaments to underlying physiological differences. More recently a very similar approach has been developed from the Jungian approach to personality which informs the rest of this book. The classical system of temperament types also forms the basis of two earlier evangelical accounts of human personality.[4]

For the *sanguine* type the dominant bodily fluid was blood. Associated with the element of air, this was the lively, buoyant temperament. Sanguine types were thought to be restless,

9

impulsive, and receptive towards their surroundings. What matters most to them is experience for its own sake rather than as a stimulus to future action. Amongst their strengths might be cited a sympathetic nature (they are naturally interested in others and able to experience with others) and a natural ability for living in the present. On the other hand the very fact that they are present-oriented can lead to a certain superficiality, inconstancy and unreliability. Anyone familiar with A. A. Milne's *The House at Pooh Corner* will recognise Tigger as a particularly bouncy example of the sanguine temperament. Kenneth Grahame's infamous Toad is another example.

Just as the opposite of air was earth, so the opposite of the sanguine temperament was the *melancholic*. This type was supposedly dominated by black bile! Melancholics are popularly supposed to be dark and gloomy. Hallesby's catalogue of the melancholic's weaknesses paints an unprepossessing portrait: he or she may be self-centred, oversensitive, uncompromising, reserved, negative, given to violent outbursts of anger, pessimistic, proud, and passive. A. A. Milne's character Eeyore, that dark and gloomy donkey, is a model melancholic.

Sadly those very public faults tend to obscure the private but very real strengths of the melancholic. They make few friends (for obvious reasons!) but are faithful and dependable. Keeping promises is a matter of personal pride. Although they are self-centred this tends to be critical rather than indulgent: they are perfectionists who are only too aware of their own limits. Indeed everything they experience tends to be judged according to some ideal standard. Not surprisingly they are deep and thorough in whatever they do.

The *choleric* temperament was dominated by yellow bile and associated with fire. As the popular usage of the word suggests, this is the hot-blooded violent temperament. But it is also the active, practical temperament. In Hallesby's words, 'To the choleric, life means more than capturing the various moods of life, or brooding over its mysteries. To him life is work, activity.'[5] Cholerics will always 'have a go'. But their activity tends to be practical and realistic. They will get on with the possible without too much concern for the unattainable ideals of the melancholic. They will persevere in the face of adversity and they are quick to respond to emergencies. On the other hand they may be lacking in compassion and they may carry through their actions with little regard for the needs or rights of others. Once again A. A. Milne provides us with an (admittedly placid) example of the choleric temperament in Rabbit.

Finally, the opposite of the choleric was the *phlegmatic* temperament. Associated with water and mucus, this was the cool, slow, sluggish type. People of a phlegmatic temperament tend to be good-natured, cosy, comfortable, and tranquil. They are calm and dependable but do tend to be slow (even lazy). That bear of little brain, Winnie-the-Pooh himself, is a classic example of the type.

The Enneagram

This is a relative newcomer in the world of personality types. Unlike the classical theory of temperaments, its origins are shrouded in mystery. Some trace it back to mediaeval Islamic mysticism, others to ancient Babylon. But in spite of this desire to give it the respectability of an ancient heritage it cannot be reliably traced back beyond the writings of the twentieth-century esoteric author, George Gurdjieff. It owes its popularity today largely to its use by the Esalen Institute (a major Californian clearing house of New Age ideas and alternative therapies) and its espousal by many American Jesuits.

According to this system of classification, everyone is a mixture of three psychological faculties: feeling, doing, and relating. Our basic personality type is determined by the one faculty which is most important in our lives.

However, this innocent self is distorted by social pressures. The dominant faculty may be distorted in one of three ways: it may be overdeveloped, underdeveloped, or we may lose touch with it altogether. This process of distortion gives rise to nine possible compulsive survival-strategies. Many Enneagram practitioners identify these with the ego. One such practitioner summarises the various strategies as follows:[6]

the helper – overdeveloped feeling
the status seeker – out of touch with feeling
the artist – underdeveloped feeling
the thinker – underdeveloped doing
the loyalist – out of touch with doing
the jack of all trades – overdeveloped doing
the leader – overdeveloped relating
the peacemaker – out of touch with relating
the reformer – underdeveloped relating

This gives a falsely static impression of the Enneagram. It is brought to life (and made considerably more complex) by the fact that these personality types are the bases from which we move. We grow by seeking to develop alternative survival strategies to complement and balance the one which has become compulsive. Thus, for example, a thinker might be encouraged to seek to become a leader.

The Enneagram is an increasingly popular tool in contemporary Christian spirituality. But like all such tools it must be used with care and, in particular, the accompanying philosophical package must be carefully scrutinised. The view of reality enshrined within the Enneagram differs from that of orthodox Christianity at a number of important points. For example, its understanding of human nature is very different from the Christian view. According to some Enneagram practitioners, a fundamentally innocent self redeems itself from the distortions imposed upon it by human society. The ultimate goal is not communion with God but with the larger self which we encounter by self-transcendence.

Jung's theory of psychological types

This third classification of human personality owes its theoretical foundation to the pioneer of depth psychology, Carl Gustav Jung. And, like the classical theory, it has already shown its worth by popularising and determining the modern meaning of two words, namely, extravert and introvert.

Jung's work on psychological types arose out of pressing practical and personal problems. At the purely practical level of his work in counselling and analysis he was very conscious of differences and even conflicts in personality. He was insistent that the analyst could never take a superior impersonal view of a patient. Successful analysis depended on the development of a genuine personal relationship between analyst and patient. Thus it was vital for the analyst to be aware of ways in which his or her personality might harmonise with, or complement, or conflict with that of the patient.

Superimposed upon this practical necessity was the problem of Jung's relationship with his older contemporary Sigmund Freud. Indeed, at one point in his autobiography, he attributes the origins of his thinking about psychological types to his need to define how his own outlook differed from that of Freud. And in later work he implies that at least part of the difference lay in the fact that Freud was an extravert who dismissed introversion as morbid self-concern while he himself was an introvert.

Apart from extraversion and introversion, the criteria he used for classifying human temperament were sensation, thinking, feeling, and intuition. He recognised that there was nothing dogmatic about this set of criteria. Others could have been used which would have resulted in very different systems. His choice was a pragmatic one, arising naturally from his own observations of human nature. In his own words,

I had always been impressed by the fact that there are a surprising number of individuals who never use their minds if they can avoid it, and an equal number who do use their

13

minds, but in an amazingly stupid way. I was also surprised to find many intelligent and wideawake people who lived (as far as one could make out) as if they had never learned to use their sense organs: They did not see the things before their eyes, hear the words sounding in their ears, or notice the things they touched or tasted. Some lived without being aware of the state of their own bodies.

There were others who seemed to live in a most curious condition of consciousness, as if the state they had arrived at today were final, with no possibility of change, or as if the world and the psyche were static and would remain so forever. They seemed devoid of all imagination, and they entirely and exclusively depended upon their sense-perception. Chances and possibilities did not exist in their world, and in 'today' there was no real 'tomorrow.' The future was just the repetition of the past.[7]

Why *four* functions? Because at a gut level Jung believed that four signified completeness. In spite of his insistence that his criteria were pragmatic rather than dogmatic, he could also say,

There are always four elements, four prime qualities, four colours, four ways of spiritual development etc. So, too, there are four aspects of psychological orientation. . . . In order to orient ourselves, we must have a function which ascertains that something is there (sensation); a second function which establishes *what* it is (thinking); a third function which states whether it suits us or not, whether we wish to accept it or not (feeling), and a fourth function which indicates where it came from and where it is going (intuition). When this has been done, there is nothing more to say.[8]

The Myers–Briggs Type Indicator

The approach to temperament adopted in this book is based largely on Jung's theory. At the turn of the century an American woman, Katharine Briggs, began informal studies of the differences in the personalities of the people around her. Like Jung she was convinced of the existence of systematic differences in the way normal people behave and the importance of these differences for human relations. Over the years she gradually developed an informal typology of human temperament.

Briggs became acquainted with Jung's work shortly after the publication of the English edition of *Psychological Types* in 1923. Seeing clear parallels with her own studies, she incorporated her own work into Jung's material. Observing psychological types in the people around them became something of a hobby for the Briggs family. In particular, this enthusiasm was shared by Katharine's daughter, Isabel Myers.

It was Isabel who conceived the notion of a questionnaire to aid people in their understanding of human temperament. Over a period of more than two decades following the Second World War she gradually built up a pool of questions designed to force respondents to choose amongst the functions and attitudes of Jung's theory. The outcome was the Myers–Briggs Type Indicator.

There is a marked difference in tone between the theory of personality types developed by Briggs and Myers and its Jungian roots. In large measure this is due to the fact that Jung developed his theory in a clinical context. His descriptions of the personality types are extreme: a single function or attitude dominates all the rest to the point where they are all inhibited or repressed. As you might expect this results in a rather negative approach to personality: Jung dwells at great length on the pathological states into which different personalities might degenerate. This is the world of hysteria and compulsion, of hypochondria and phobia, of neurosis and psychosis.

By contrast the Myers–Briggs Type Indicator paints a very positive picture of the differences in human temperament. Their aim was to enable the normal person to understand

15

better his or her temperament rather than to enable the clinical psychologist to understand those of his patients.

Talking Temperament: Vocabulary

The Myers–Briggs Type Indicator (or MBTI) is designed to indicate our preferences on four scales: extraversion (E) or introversion (I); sensing (S) or intuition (N); thinking (T) or feeling (F); and, judgement (J) or perception (P). The first three scales measure those preferences which, according to Jung, have a significant effect on the way in which we look at the world and act on what we see. The fourth was added during the development of the Myers–Briggs Type Indicator in order to make explicit certain features of Jung's theory which he had not developed.

ATTITUDES TO THE WORLD

The first scale of the Myers–Briggs Type Indicator is *Extraversion* (E) or *Introversion* (I). Some questions in the Indicator are calculated to make us choose between the outer world of objects and people and the inner world of ideas and feelings. We all have to live in both worlds but, according to Jung's theory, we tend to exhibit a consistent preference for one or the other. A helpful comparison is that with our tendency to be left or right-handed. Although we have two hands, we generally show a marked preference for one rather than the other. Even the ambidextrous minority is likely to prefer one hand in some situations and the other in different situations. So it is with the choices in the Myers–Briggs Type Indicator: all of us possess and can use both faculties but we tend to prefer one rather than the other.

The person who coined the phrase, 'Don't just stand there, do something!' was probably an extravert. And if the person he was addressing was an introvert she might have retorted that she was doing something: she was busy mulling over all the possible courses of action and their short, medium, and long-term consequences. Except, of course, that, as an introvert, she is more likely to think that and feel resentful about the extravert's comment than set the record straight.

Extraverted behaviour is focussed on the outer world, on people and things. It is responsive to its physical, social, and cultural environment. Its chief characteristic is practical activity.

Introverted behaviour looks inwards towards our thoughts, feelings, impressions, and mental images. When behaving in this way we may be completely oblivious to our surroundings. We are reflective rather than active.

The stereotypical extravert is someone who is consistently drawn outwards by external claims and conditions. He or she enjoys action, people, busyness, the hustle and bustle of modern city life. Because of this preference they appear to be relaxed and confident in the midst of all that is going on around them.

An extravert will tend to act first and think about the consequences of their action later. They are naturally given to a trial and error approach to life. This extends to their personal relationships where they are likely to speak without weighing every word. As a result they appear talkative and friendly; they are easy to get to know. But by the same token they may seem superficial (particularly to introverts).

Not only do extraverts speak (or act) before thinking, they will speak in order to find out what they think. 'How do I know what I think until I hear myself say it', is a characteristically extravert statement. Lawrence once found himself being consulted frequently by an extravert colleague. It soon became clear that he was not interested in getting Lawrence's opinions but was using him as a sounding board in order to formulate his own views and policies.

As you might expect, the stereotypical introvert is the opposite of all this. He or she finds the claims of the external world intrusive rather than attractive. Given the chance they will seek to escape from the noise and activity of the city. This escape need not be physical because for an introvert the true direction of escape is inwards. Thus they may appear to hold other people and external claims on their time and energies at arm's length: they come across as reserved, even taciturn.

Whereas the extravert thrives on relationships and action the introvert values peace and solitude. He or she is not anti-social but prefers one or two close friendships to a lively social life and a host of acquaintances. Too many people and too much activity soon drives an introvert to distraction. One of the minor irritations in our marriage is a direct result of this difference between extraverts and introverts. Diana (an extravert) will see something that requires action and say so, but then she will see something else, and something else, and so on. Lawrence (an introvert) will respond (more or less happily) to the first suggestion. But just as he is in the middle of one thing he will be interrupted. . . . Very soon he is uttering the introvert's favourite *cri de coeur*, 'Just one thing at a time please!'

The introvert's preferred world is the inner world of ideas, feelings, and mental images. Often they will have well-developed fantasy worlds within: worlds with their own consistency and populations. The poet Hopkins spoke of this as an inscape and like the physical world it can be awe-inspiring possessing 'cliffs of fall, no man fathom'd'.

The introvert will always reflect before acting or speaking. As a result he or she may appear to possess greater intellectual depth than an extravert of similar intelligence. However, the impression of depth may go hand in hand with a tendency towards impracticality. The introvert may get so carried away with reflecting about what to do or say that the action is never taken, the words are never spoken. Lawrence frequently finds in discussion that he will come up with the perfect response to someone's point only to find that while he has been thinking about it the conversation has moved on to something quite different. For this reason introverts may prefer to communicate through writing rather than speech: it slows the exchange down sufficiently for them to be able to give a considered response.

The introvert's preference for the written word and the extravert's preference for discussion may be combined in creative ways. In fact, the evolution of this book is an example of how that might happen. Lawrence worked out his ideas on paper before conferring with Diana. As an extravert, the discussion was the point at which she began to generate ideas of her own to modify Lawrence's written notes.

The stereotypes give a clear picture of what we mean by extravert and introvert. But they are only stereotypes. We should never make the mistake of assuming that a person's preference limits him or her to the behaviour we expect of the stereotype. Just as a right-handed person can learn to use their left hand effectively so an extravert can learn to be reflective, can learn to value their inner world. Conversely an introvert can learn the social skills that come naturally to the extravert. Indeed it can be argued that an important part of personal development involves learning those skills and behaviours that do not seem to come naturally. The benefit to an introvert of learning social skills is obvious. The benefits of learning to be reflective are less obvious but no less real.

But, however much one learns, a natural preference will remain. That preference is likely to reassert itself when the person is under pressure. If you throw a tomato at a right-handed person they will probably try to ward it off with their right hand. If you force an extravert to take a thirty-day silent retreat they will probably emerge desperate to immerse themselves once more in the busyness of the city. Diana has learned to appreciate the value of silent retreats but, nevertheless, returns to the world of relationships and activity with a sense of relief.

Conversely, if you force an introvert into an active social or business life they will probably need to escape from time to time. An incident from the Old Testament displays this rather well. In 1 Kings 18, God orders Elijah to come out of seclusion and confront the political and religious establishment of Israel. Elijah obeys and confronts several hundred pagan prophets before the assembled multitude on Mount Carmel. His actions are crowned with success, the king is humbled, the false prophets are butchered, the drought ends, and yet when the queen threatens him, Elijah's nerve finally snaps. All he can think of is escape from these crowds: he runs away and hides himself in the wilderness of Sinai (where he can once more hear the voice of God in the stillness and solitude of that place).

WAYS OF LOOKING AT THE WORLD

Jung's theory suggests that there are two main ways of perceiving our worlds (both inner and outer): *sensing* (S) and *intuition* (N). These make up the second preference scale of the Myers–Briggs Type Indicator.

Sensing is self-explanatory: information is obtained directly through the five senses. Eyes, ears, nose, tongue, and touch tell you what is happening. In case we are tempted to take our senses for granted, it is worth recalling that they are capable of incredible feats of discrimination. For example, the Nobel prize-winning physicist, Richard Feynman, has written of his prowess as a human bloodhound:

I went out again, she took a book, opened it and closed it, and put it back. I came in – and nothing *to* it! It was easy. You just smell the books. It's hard to explain, because we're not used to saying things about it. You put each book up to your nose and sniff a few times, and you can tell. It's very different. A book that's been standing there a while has a dry, uninteresting kind of smell. But when a hand has touched it, there's a dampness and smell that's very distinct.[1]

Intuition is less obvious. Many people will immediately qualify it with the adjective 'female' and dismiss it as nothing more than the entertainment of irrational hunches. Others celebrate intuition as a mysterious psychological faculty capable of offering us insights superior to those of the intellect. Jung (and the Myers–Briggs Type Indicator) offers a much more satisfactory account of intuition than either of these. Notice first of all that intuition is not the opposite of thinking: it performs a completely different function. Its opposite is sensing and like sensing it should complement rather than compete with the way we make our decisions.

What then is intuition? Most people now accept that the conscious mind is only the tip of a psychological iceberg. The part of me that is aware that I am me is only part of my soul. The incontrovertible fact that we dream points to the existence of other less accessible places within our souls.[2] Briefly, intuition is the processing of sense information through the unconscious levels of the soul. Information from the senses is combined with memories, images, and associations to produce anything from a mere hunch to the creative insight which can open up a new field of science or result in a great work of art.

As with extraversion and introversion, the Myers–Briggs Type Indicator elicits your preference for either sensing or intuition. And, as before, the fact that you prefer one of these ways of seeing does not preclude your using the other.

Sensing (S)

What is the characteristic behaviour of the person who prefers sensing? Good development of the sensing function results in a person who is observant, who has a refined awareness of present experience, who finds it relatively easy to remember details and facts. A sensing person sees the world as it is. He or she is likely to be regarded as a person with their feet firmly on the ground, a realist.

Of the authors, Diana is a typical sensing type. She is acutely conscious of the state of the home. On entering a room she will immediately register that a picture is askew, the coffee cups haven't been tidied away, and Lawrence has forgotten to dust the bookshelves.

This combination of abilities has some clear implications for a person's temperament. Sensing people, because of their sensitivity to present reality, are inclined to be pleasure-loving and present-oriented. They enjoy life as it is. Thus they are likely to be contented with the status quo and reluctant to sacrifice the reality of present enjoyment for the possibility of some future good. 'A bird in the hand is worth two in the bush' sums up this implication of a preference for sensing. This also issues in a preference for stability and tradition: sensing types are the natural conservatives of society.

The sensing type's facility with facts and details means that he or she is good at following instructions. However, any old instructions won't do. The acute powers of observation result in an expectation that facts will be exact (after all they can observe with uncanny accuracy) and instructions will be clear.

A less obvious implication is an expectation that meetings will produce results. Sensing types are interested in concrete realities in this world. A meeting which fails to ground itself in reality will be seen as a waste of time.

Clearly overdependence on the sensing function can produce its own characteristic set of faults. If it is not balanced by the appropriate use of one of the judging functions, the sensing type's enjoyment of the present can degenerate into frivolity and hedonism. Similarly a stress on sensing at the expense of intuition can result in an unimaginative approach to life. The Dickensian teacher for whom a horse was merely a quadrapedal beast of burden typifies this outlook: hard facts are the only reality; if you can't precisely quantify it, it doesn't exist.

Intuition (N)

And what of the person who displays a consistent preference for intuition? Good development of this function results in a capacity to find patterns and relationships in even very complex situations. Nor is this pattern-seeking confined to the present. It leads naturally to a tendency to extrapolate from present realities to future possibilities. This is the type of perception that is fundamental to sound strategic thinking. One might expect good chess players to make use of intuition while they are considering the consequences of all the possible moves that are open to them. It is also typical of mathematicians, research scientists and creative thinkers of all sorts.

But if intuition is to flower into genuine creativity it must be backed up by appropriate use of other functions. Otherwise it evaporates in the mere daydreaming of a Billy Liar or a Walter Mitty.

The intuitive can only too easily leave his or her less imaginative colleagues gasping with bewilderment by making apparently illogical jumps from A to X. For the sensing type an apple is a piece of fruit with a certain colour, weight, texture, flavour. For the intuitive it is the gateway to an open-ended collection of memories, images, associations. It may conjure up stories of William Tell which may in turn lead the intuitive to think about nationalism, or the operas of Rossini, or Swiss clocks, or Swiss banks!

There is an apocryphal story which illustrates the hazards of intuition very well: A mathematician is in the midst of a lecture. He writes down an equation, says, 'It is intuitively obvious that . . .' and writes down the next line. He pauses, looks at his working, mutters, 'Excuse me, gentlemen' and leaves the lecture theatre. Twenty minutes later he returns with a sheaf of hastily scribbled notes and triumphantly announces to the class, 'Yes, gentlemen, it *is* intuitively obvious!'

The future-orientation of the intuitive may show itself in other ways. Possibilities may be more interesting than realities, the future more interesting than the present. The intuitive is less dependent on his or her physical environment than the sensing type. They are also more likely to be dissatisfied with the status quo: there are always ways in which matters could be improved. Intuitives are more likely to be reformers, radicals, and revolutionaries. They value change and novelty. If taken to extremes (and not balanced by a developed judging function) novelty may become their ultimate value: they may become fickle, lacking the persistence needed to bring a project to a successful conclusion. When turned upon themselves this preference for future possibilities may well generate a hundred ways in which they could do better. Perfectionism is one of the besetting sins of the intuitive. Again it needs to be balanced by a judging function. Lawrence sees this in his own approach to writing: only deadlines imposed by himself, Diana, and their publishers enable him to put pen to paper. And when the finished product reaches the shops he is painfully aware of ways in which it could have been improved.

As regards facts, theories and instructions intuitives take quite a different line from sensing types. Facts are always merely approximate. Theories are more important than facts. The physicist who, when told that his theory did not agree with the observations, retorted, 'So much the worse for the facts!' was certainly an intuitive. That attitude may sound profoundly unscientific but, in fact, it is quite widespread amongst theoretical scientists and philosophers. In the past it has led to scandalous distortions of science (e.g., Soviet biology's domination by the erroneous theories of Lysenko) but it has also enabled theoretical scientists to refute erroneous observations!

When it comes to following instructions, the intuitive is likely to get into trouble with the sensing type. Sensing types follow (and expect others to follow) instructions meticulously. Intuitives rapidly get bored with instruction manuals and begin to experiment. It seems obvious that if you do this and this you will get that result. As you might imagine this can easily lead to problems. The authors once had a major row which was the

25

direct result of just such a difference over an instruction manual. Diana asked Lawrence to show her how to use their new word processor. As a sensing type, she expected him to talk her through the instruction manual step by step. As an intuitive he had ignored the instruction manual since the day they had first unpacked the computer. Within a matter of minutes, Lawrence was reduced to a state of total frustration by Diana's seemingly wilful refusal to grasp things that were just obvious. Meanwhile Diana was rapidly losing her temper over Lawrence's wilful refusal to explain things in logical steps which bore some relation to the instructions in the manual. It so happened that just a few days later Diana went on a basic Myers–Briggs workshop. She returned enthusing about the Indicator and exclaiming that now she understood why we had that row! We had discovered that the Myers–Briggs Type Indicator was a very practical tool for helping us to improve our understanding of each other.

Finally, a preference for intuition may result in a very different kind of business meeting from that enjoyed by sensing types. For intuitives it is not enough for meetings to produce the concrete results coveted by sensing types. Such results are only of value if they have been preceded by discussions which go to the roots of the matter.

Two Ways of Making Decisions

The third scale of the Myers–Briggs Type Indicator examines our preference within the second pair of psychological functions described by Jung's theory: *thinking* (T) and *feeling* (F). These are essentially two very different approaches to decision making though their implications for our temperaments go far beyond mere decision making.

Thinking (T)

Judgement based on thinking is self-explanatory. Choices are made on the basis of impersonal logical criteria (or cause and effect). Decisions can be right or wrong; true or false.

Good development of the thinking function is apparent in a person's capacity for objective analysis of situations and theories. The aspects of a person's temperament associated with the development of thinking are objectivity, impartiality, and a sense of fairness and justice.

The objectivity of the thinking type is perhaps his or her most visible characteristic. 'Thinkers' see things from the outside. They are spectators of life rather than participants. At times, when feelings are running high, this can be a valuable trait. 'If you can keep your head, when all about are losing theirs . . .' you are probably a 'thinker'.

On other occasions, such a calm detached outlook can be a liability. When what is required is warmth and sympathy, thinking behaviour can come across as cold and unsympathetic.

The 'thinker's' preference for logic may also be expressed in a tendency to be truthful rather than tactful. 'What do you think of my new hat/latest painting/new idea?' may be a request for appreciation rather than impersonal analysis. The 'thinker' is more likely to offer the latter. Thus he or she appears to be spontaneously critical. If this is taken to extremes the 'thinker' appears carping, nit-picking, always quick to find fault with others.

Feeling (F)

In contrast to thinking, feeling is only too easily misunderstood. Part of the problem lies in the translation of Jung's theory from German to English. Feeling suggests to us irrationality as opposed to the rationality of thinking. So a feeling type would be irrational, emotional, possibly sentimental. However, Jung was insistent that both thinking and feeling are rational functions.

The difference between them is not the difference between reason and unreason. On the contrary, both thinking and feeling are sound bases for rational judgements. Rather the difference lies in the criteria on which the judgements are based. Thinking prefers objective criteria: the laws of logic, cause and effect, etc. Feeling judgements are based on more subjective criteria: ethical norms (though, of course, thinking types also have a calculus of morality), aesthetic criteria, personal and social needs. For feeling types decisions are good or bad rather than true or false.

There is a common misapprehension that science is exclusively concerned with the impersonal rational judgements associated with thinking. In fact this is not the case. Feeling judgements often play an important part in the choice between competing scientific theories. Scientists often rely on aesthetic criteria rather than logical ones when choosing between theories. Considerations of elegance and simplicity fall firmly in the sphere of feeling rather than thinking judgements.

A corollary of this subjective basis for decision making is a tendency to be involved rather than detached. Feeling types are committed participants rather than detached observers. The participation is an essential part of their being able to make appropriate decisions.

Where the thinking type is critical the feeling type is appreciative. They are concerned with harmony and good personal relationships rather than truth and impersonal justice. When asked 'What do you think of . . .' they are likely to take account of the feelings of the other person and respond tactfully.

For the feeling type, truth and justice have an ineradicable personal element. A truth that tramples down someone's sensibilities cannot be the whole truth. They will be quick to remind us that the Bible commands that we speak the truth *in love*. Similarly justice cannot be impersonal. If it does not take account of the persons it affects, it is not genuine justice.

Clearly, thinking and feeling must be complementary rather than mutually exclusive if we are to be fully human. Thinking alone may make a person seem cold and uncaring. Feeling alone may lead a person to over-commit themselves to a particular cause (the first step on the road to fanaticism). Being able to use the opposite function when necessary is a valuable source of balance.

PERCEIVING OR JUDGING?

Each pair of the psychological functions described above has a collective name. Together, sensing and intuition are known as the *perceiving functions* since they refer to the ways we look at or perceive our world. Thinking and feeling are called the *judging functions* since they refer to the ways in which we make decisions.

The final scale of the Myers–Briggs Type Indicator relates to a factor which is left implicit in Jung's theory. Not only did Jung argue that we show a preference for one or other of the perceiving and judging functions, but he suggested that we tend to use just one of these functions in our dealings with the external world. The JP-scale is based on questions which elicit whether we prefer to use our judging function (thinking or feeling) or our perceiving function (sensing or intuition) in the outside world.

According to type theorists, this preference for judging or perceiving results in some of the most marked differences in human temperament.

A judging temperament is essentially one that approaches the external world by making decisions about it. Structure is important. Their lifestyle and their environment must be organised by social convention, tradition, customs, bureaucratic rulebook, or their own plans. The external world must be kept under control. One personal example of this was the meals rota we devised at a time when we were both engaged in demanding full-time work: after a particularly bad week in which we were reduced to eating cheese on toast at several meals in a row, we sat down and devised a monthly cycle of meals (together with a note of who would be responsible for which meals).

Mediaeval monks believed that land which lacked a discernible structure imposed by agriculture was accursed wilderness. Judging types feel much the same way about time. For them, unstructured time is time wasted.

Since both of us are judging types this is a very strong feature of our household. The most recent example of this outlook is the timetable we drew up for the Christmas holidays. We planned activities to keep our daughter amused and stimulated throughout the holiday period.

Judging types also like matters to be settled. Periods of uncertainty are times of great anxiety. In our experience job-hunting and house-buying are particularly trying precisely because we are not in complete control.

This need for control may make it difficult for judging types to delegate responsibility to others. At times they may be inclined to jump to conclusions without adequately assessing the situation. Or they may give the impression that they have already decided what others ought to do. Their reliance on the diary may also give their lives a certain rigidity. For example, in the past Lawrence has succumbed to the temptation to regiment his day to such an extent that the unexpected simply could not be handled. Such weaknesses highlight the need for a developed perceiving function to offset the tendency to control everything in sight.

As you can imagine, judging types are much in demand in our busy society. They are the men and women who extol the virtues of time management (and put it into practice).

A tendency to approach life with the perceiving function (whether sensing or intuition) leads to a very different temperament. Perceiving types are experience-oriented rather than goal-oriented. Instead of trying to keep everything under control, they are hungry for new experiences.

Perceiving types thrive on open-endedness. They enjoy experiencing new situations. As a result they are more inclined to be genuinely interested in what people are in fact doing than in deciding what they ought to do.

Their aim in life is to miss nothing of the tremendous richness that is unfolding around them. Thus, at their best, perceiving types are flexible, open and tolerant. They are happy to let be and observe.

However, if this is not balanced by a developed judging function, this emphasis on sheer enjoyment of experience can lead to indecision. There are always new facts and new factors that could affect our decisions. Therefore the moment of decision is continually put off.

Such indecision may be acceptable if you work alone. However, it can prove immensely troublesome for people who are awaiting your decisions. Judging types, in particular, find it very irksome. Diana (a typical judging type) still shudders when she recalls a particular incident involving a perceiving clergyman. She was due to assist him during a Sunday morning service but she received no indication of what he expected her to do. On the morning of the service they gathered in the vestry and, as the choir began to file into the church, he turned to her and said, 'I think you can preach this morning.'

Exercises

(a) Eat an apple[3]

This is a simple exercise to encourage the use of all four psychological functions. You will need a notepad and an eating apple. Head four pages in turn: Sensing, Intuition, Feeling, Thinking.

Now begin eating the apple slowly. As you eat, take two or

three minutes to concentrate on each of the functions in turn listing what comes to mind as you do so.

(1) List your sense impressions. Try to pay attention to every detail. Note the colours, textures, shapes, tastes, and smells of the various parts of the apple. You might also focus on the process of eating: the muscular movements, etc.

(2) What intuitions does the process of eating an apple evoke? What memories or associations do you recall? Does it remind you of anyone? What about apples in stories, myths, or traditions?

(3) How did you feel about this experiment? What feelings were evoked by eating this apple?

(4) Can you make any logical deductions about this apple from your sense impressions or intuitions? What conclusions can you draw about apples in general?

Although the exercise can be done individually, it is greatly enhanced by doing it in a group. By comparing our responses with those of others we are brought face to face with some of the psychological differences which exist in any group of people.

(b) Type watching

The Myers–Briggs Type Indicator grew out of informal attempts to match Jung's theory to behaviour observed in everyday life. This is still an excellent way to familiarise yourself with type theory.

As you read through the chapter you will no doubt have thought of friends, relatives or colleagues who behave in ways which are typical of one or other of the preferences. You might like to systematise those reflections by creating your own personal type chart indicating people whom you regard as typical of each of these preferences.

The practical value of such an exercise is twofold. It enables you to get a better grasp of type theory by making it personal and concrete. But, more importantly, it gives you a basis for beginning to look for ways to improve your relationships with the people who appear on your list. For example, you may recall disagreements or misunderstandings which now appear to have arisen because of type differences. In the light of type theory, what practical steps could you take to avoid such misunderstandings in the future?

If you do undertake this exercise you should remember one thing: type is not a prison; it should not be used to pigeonhole people and predict their behaviour. One of the fundamental characteristics of human beings is their capacity to surprise us.

Talking Temperament: Grammar

So far we have examined the eight preferences that make up the Myers–Briggs Type Indicator. Hopefully you will already have begun to see how these fit together to create a particularly rich and fruitful way of talking about human temperament. But if we were to stop at that point we would have only half the story.

As the titles of this and the previous chapter suggest we believe that the Myers–Briggs Type Indicator offers a useful language with which to speak about some of the ways in which we differ from one another.

If you like, the eight preferences provide us with the vocabulary for this way of talking about temperament. But vocabulary is only half a language: it enables us to begin to understand and make ourselves understood. But if we are to go any further we must also have some knowledge of the grammar, of how the words are combined into sentences and paragraphs. Similarly the next step in understanding Jung's theory of psychological types is to look at how the eight preferences combine. In all they can be combined in sixteen different ways to give us that number of distinct temperament types. The purpose of this chapter is to put the terms together and show how they interact in different combinations.

The 16 types[1]

| ISTJ | ISFJ | INFJ | INTJ |
| ISTP | ISFP | INFP | INTP |

| ESTP | ESFP | ENFP | ENTP |
| ESTJ | ESFJ | ENFJ | ENTJ |

THE INTERRELATIONSHIP OF OUR PREFERENCES

At the heart of Jung's work on personality is a theory about the ways in which we combine the four psychological functions: sensing, intuition, thinking, and feeling. The other preference scales used by the Indicator tell us important facts about our attitude to the inner and outer worlds: facts which enable us to determine in what circumstances we are likely to use the four functions.

Many people misunderstand the Myers–Briggs Type Indicator at this point. They think that a preference for one function implies that they are unable to use its complement. Thus Lawrence might use the fact that he is an intuitive to excuse the untidiness of his study: he just doesn't notice the details (like that pile of papers and books on the floor by his desk). Unfortunately for Lawrence, Jung's theory assumes that everyone *is* capable of exercising all four functions.

We enter this world with the capacity to perceive via senses *and* intuition, and to make decisions on the basis of both thinking *and* feeling. However, somewhere along the line we develop a preference for one or other of each pair. And we also develop a preference for either the inner or the outer world. But these are only *preferences*. The untidiness of Lawrence's study is not because he is incapable of applying his sensing function to his immediate environment. Rather it arises because he chooses not to do so: he cannot use his Jungian type as a way of evading his responsibilities.

The origin of our preferences

Just how this development of preferences arises is open to debate. Jung himself, together with many Jungians and type theorists, assumed that it arose largely from a genetic disposition: thus the analogy of handedness used earlier could be more than a helpful illustration.

On the other hand it is clear that all sorts of external circumstances conspire to push us in particular directions. It is no coincidence that in the usual layout of the Myers–Briggs Type Indicator the preferences on the left are stereotypically masculine while those on the right are stereotypically feminine:

Extravert	Introvert
Sensing	iNtuitive
Thinking	Feeling
Judging	Perceiving

Sexual stereotypes, racial and cultural factors are all recognised as having a part to play in determining our temperament. However, belief in the priority of a genetic predisposition leads to the belief that we have a 'true' personality type. This, in turn, causes some users of the Myers–Briggs Type Indicator to regard such external factors as entirely negative. If nurture reinforces what nature has given us all well and good: but it is still nature which takes the credit. If nature and nurture come into conflict then it is assumed that our nurture must be at fault. The practical outcome is that many practitioners encourage their clients to seek a true self which may have been suppressed by their childhood submission to the expectations of parents, peers, and authoritative others.

This is one point at which Christians may want to differ from type theory. If we take the doctrine of the Trinity seriously, we will insist that the very essence of being human lies in our being in free personal relationships with one another and with

God. Thus we will agree with Jung that we are free to exercise all our God-given psychological functions (the ones highlighted by Jung and all the others besides). But we may well be wary of the priority which is apparently given to genetics at this point.

A hierarchy of preferences

But whatever the source of our preferences it is clear from observing the way we behave that we do, in fact, display such preferences. Jung and those who have followed him discern a more or less clear hierarchy within each person's use of the four psychological functions. The hierarchy comes about by the simple fact that our preferences tend to be self-reinforcing. If we use one function in preference to its complement we are likely to develop greater skill in the use of that function. This in turn will lead to a stronger preference for that function.

Again the analogy of handedness is useful: the very fact that a child prefers to use one hand rather than the other will mean that he or she gets more practice in the use of that hand. What may have started out as a slight preference will gradually become much stronger. Our eldest child appeared to be completely ambidextrous as a toddler. Four years on, she will still sometimes use her left hand for writing and drawing but her preference for the right hand has become much more pronounced.

The function you prefer to use with your favoured world (outer if you are extravert; inner if you are introvert) is likely to be the one that is most highly developed. Thus you are likely to be most comfortable when exercising this function. It is the function you find most interesting and, of course, it is the one you are most likely to turn to; the one you are most likely to rely upon. Not surprising, then, that it is usually described as your *dominant* function. And, of course, it will be one of the two functions listed in your type formula.

The other function that appears in your type formula is your second choice of function (usually called the *auxiliary* function). It is developed as a balance to the dominant function and, according to type theory, is also likely to be used chiefly in our less preferred world.

What about the functions which do not appear in your type formula? These are the functions which you have not chosen. The fact that you prefer the other functions may indicate that you find these functions less interesting; you may feel less comfortable when you have to exercise one of these functions. Perhaps you tend to neglect one or both of them.

But, given our type formula (the four letters which denote our preferences on the Myers–Briggs Type Indicator), how can we work out which functions we will use in particular circumstances?

The place to begin is with the JP-scale. This indicates which function you prefer to use when relating to the outside world. If it is J, then you prefer to use a judging function (T or F). If it is P, you tend to use a perceiving function (S or N).

For extraverts, the function indicated by their JP preference is their dominant function (the function they prefer to use in their preferred world). For introverts, this function is their auxiliary (because the outer world is *not* their preferred world).

Diana is an ESFJ. Her preference for judging implies that feeling (her judging function) will be dominant, the one she tends to use most (and most effectively) in her preferred world. The other function cited in her type formula is sensing. This is her auxiliary.

Lawrence is an INTJ. He relies on his judging function in relating to the outer world. But, because he is an introvert, his judging function (thinking) will be his auxiliary *not* his dominant function. The other function in his type formula, intuition, is the one he prefers to use in his preferred world, i.e., it is his dominant function.

Continuing the hierarchy, your third favourite (sometimes called the *tertiary* function) will be the complement of your auxiliary function. In Diana's case, since sensing is her auxiliary function intuition will be her tertiary function. And your least favourite function, probably the least developed of all, will be the complement of your dominant (most developed) function. For Lawrence this will be sensing, since his dominant function is intuition.

THE SIXTEEN PSYCHOLOGICAL TYPES

The simplest way of describing how the psychological functions and attitudes interact is to offer descriptions of each of the types identified by the Myers–Briggs Type Indicator. For the sake of clarity, we shall group these into the eight categories originally described by Jung.

Extraverted thinking types (E _ TJ)

These are the extraverts for whom thinking is the dominant function. In other words they tend, whenever possible, to apply rational logical decision-making processes to the world around them. They like to be in control and their control will be characterised by a tendency to impersonal efficiency. Decisive and disciplinarian, they are people who get things done. Isabel Briggs Myers has described them as 'the standard executive type'.[2] They are effective because they tend to be as tough on themselves as they are on anyone else.

As judging types, they tend to live by rules. Those rules are subject only to principles of reason. If you want to change an extraverted thinker you must do so by rational argument.

Because thinking is their favourite psychological function its complementary function, feeling, may be given little exercise. This may manifest itself in a tendency to neglect personal relationships or aesthetic activities. Since decisions are based on purely logical criteria their ethical implications may be over-looked. Occasionally feeling may be repressed to the point where it erupts in invective against those with whom we disagree. Jung described the outcome thus: 'Truth is no longer allowed to speak for itself; it is identified with the subject and treated like a sensitive darling whom an evil-minded critic has wronged. The critic is demolished, if possible with personal invective, and no argument is too gross to be used against him.'[3]

One of the perceiving functions will be used as the auxiliary to balance thinking. If the auxiliary is sensing (ESTJ) the person is likely to be down-to-earth, practical, concerned with facts about present realities. They are fascinated by new things which appeal directly to the senses: the latest gadget, new physical activities, new people to meet, new places to visit. If thinking is combined with intuition (ENTJ) their interest in future possibilities is likely to be heightened. They are also likely to be more interested in new ideas, theories, and concepts than their sensing counterpart.

The former is likely to make a highly efficient administrator, capable of keeping daily business running smoothly. The latter, while competent at that level, may show greater aptitude for strategic planning.

Extraverted feeling types (E _ FJ)

Like the extraverted thinkers, these types of people approach the world around them through their judging function: they like to be in control of things. However, their approach to decision-making and control is completely different to that of the thinkers. Instead of attempting to make the world around them subject to reason, they exert control by seeking to achieve social harmony.

At their best, such people radiate warmth. They approach life on a very personal level; they are sensitive to the needs of the other person. One such person recently commented to us that 'I am being true to myself when I please people.'

The desire for social harmony may well lead the extraverted feeling type to bolster up the status quo. Jung saw this type as one mainstay of traditional values. For example, writing about the extraverted feeling type's approach to romance, Jung says, 'the "suitable" man is loved, and no one else; he is suitable not because he appeals to her hidden subjective nature . . . but because he comes up to all reasonable expectations in the matter of age, position, income, size and respectability of his family, etc.'[4]

This may sound cold and calculating but in fact this type does not arrive at his or her conclusion by a process of impersonal analysis. Rather it is that the objective facts are the very stuff of which social harmony is constructed: these are the factors which are valued in this society, therefore these are sought as objective benchmarks of harmony. Jung quotes one such person as having told him, 'But I can't think what I don't feel.'[5]

Taken to extremes such a person may be very much at the mercy of his or her peer group. Because they need to feel that things are settled they may too readily adapt to the demands of those around them.

As with the extraverted thinker, sensing or intuition provides a balance to the feeling function. In the case of sensing (ESFJ), this may heighten the tendency to look for specific objective factors to anchor feeling in the external world. At one level this may result in a tendency to be fashion conscious. At a deeper level, Jung saw this as an essential foundation for the support of key cultural institutions.

The combination of intuition with extraverted feeling (ENFJ) may result in a charismatic visionary personality. Such people appear to see further than the rest of us and because of their sensitivity to their audience are better able than most to draw others into their vision of reality.

Extraverted sensation types (ES_P)

Extraverts who approach the world primarily through the five senses are, as you would expect, likely to be keenly observant.

41

Ultimately the world of the five senses exists for their enjoyment.

Their great capacity for enjoyment means that they are likely to be good company. This is reinforced by the fact that they are not likely to expect others to conform to their view of reality: they are likely to be among the most tolerant of personality types.

Their sensitivity to the material world may enable them to develop a very refined aesthetic sense. Style and good taste may well be second nature to such people. One would expect a study of the world's gastronomes and wine connoisseurs to reveal an unusually high proportion of this type. Turning to the more mundane level of work, such people may be attracted to jobs which enable them to apply their expert sensing. For example, they may enjoy the precise manipulation of delicate pieces of machinery. They are born craftsmen rather than production line workers. That craftsmanship may be applied to the playing of a musical instrument or the extreme delicacy of neurosurgery.

Of course the dangers of exaggerating this personality type will be obvious to anyone within the Christian tradition. In such cases the world exists merely to satisfy their craving for sensation. Two of the seven deadly sins (i.e., lust and gluttony) are directly related to just this sort of over-indulgence in material realities.

As a balance to sensation, this type will prefer either thinking or feeling. If their auxiliary function is thinking (ESTP), the rationality of their decision-making processes may mitigate their dominant tendency to be easy-going. They are likely to be more analytical, more conscious of the logical consequences of acts or decisions. On the other hand, feeling as an auxiliary function (ESFP) results in a personality type which is characterised above all by friendliness. Their interest is focussed on people and they have years of experience in handling human contacts in a tactful and easy manner. They may also have a well-developed artistic judgement.

Extraverted intuitive types (EN _ P)

These people tend to approach the world around them primarily through intuition. The single most important thing in their lives is novelty. Nothing suffocates them more effectively than a stable traditional environment. They will be in the forefront of anything that seems new or exciting, anything that has potential. Jung once said of them (and other intuitives), 'Emerging possibilities are compelling motives from which intuition cannot escape, and to which all else must be sacrificed.'[6]

If they are loyal to anything it will be to their own vision of how things might be. As a result they may be tempted to ride roughshod over others in order to realise their vision. On the other hand, lacking the desire for control of the judging types, such people are more susceptible to new visions. They may rapidly tire of the cause they have been championing and move on to new territory, leaving others to pick up the pieces or reap the harvest.

Their lives tend to be marked by a series of projects. If this is understood it may be possible for them (or someone counselling them) to build that sequence into a coherent pattern. But this will demand perseverance. A real danger for this type is the temptation to move onto a new project at the first sign of difficulties. Isabel Briggs Myers suggests that, 'It is not quitting if an intuitive woman writes one good mystery and stops because mystery writing is not what she wants to do the rest of her life; but it *is* quitting if she stops in the middle or finishes badly what she could finish well.'[7]

Another necessity is discrimination. Faced with the myriad possibilities of this world, an intuitive may never get started. A developed auxiliary function is vital here; for extraverted intuitives it will be a judging function (precisely what is needed to provide that element of discrimination). If their auxiliary is thinking (ENTP) they will tend to be more analytical and impersonal. If it is feeling (ENFP) they will be more concerned with people and their intuitive powers may give them a natural advantage in counselling.

Introverted thinking types (I _ TP)

Like the extraverted thinker, thinking is dominant. However, it is directed inwards rather than outwards. Thus his or her thinking will be concerned not with facts in the real world but with views, questions, theories, or insights. Facts may well be permitted as illustrations of the theory but they are never gathered for their own sake.

Jung cited two of the great names in German philosophy as typical of this personality type: Kant and Nietzsche. The former argued very convincingly that the human mind imposed structure on an otherwise chaotic reality. The latter ended his days in a lunatic asylum, his understanding of reality having come into fatal conflict with reality itself! Beyond the temptation of twisting the facts to fit the theory lies the danger of ignoring the facts altogether in pursuit of a personal fantasy.

As we noted earlier Briggs Myers went beyond Jung's original work in highlighting the importance of the auxiliary function. She suggested that it acts as a balance to the dominant function and is exercised chiefly in relation to the individual's less preferred world. This is doubly important for introverts because their less preferred world is the world of everyday life.

In the case of introverted thinkers they will tend to approach everyday life through their preferred perceptive process: sensing or intuition. Thus they may appear quiet, curious about the world around them in a detached way, and fairly adaptable. Only with their close friends is their thinking likely to come to the fore. Otherwise this may only make itself apparent when one of their principles is violated: under such circumstances usually adaptable people may suddenly dig their heels in and become quite intractable.

Those whose auxiliary function is sensing (ISTP) may come across as quieter versions of the extraverted sensation type.

They are realistic and have a great capacity for facts and details. With their hidden but dominant thinking function they find that work involving the analysis of masses of confused data appeals to them.

Where intuition is the auxiliary (INTP), they are likely to show a lively interest in possibilities and speculation. They may be attracted to philosophy or other areas demanding abstract thought.

In both cases feeling is likely to be their least developed function. Combined with their introversion this can make for someone who appears aloof or detached.

Introverted feeling types (I_FP)

Once again feeling is dominant but in this case it is introverted. Such people do not usually give the impression of being warm human beings. Jung described them as silent, inscrutable, and cool. Like the extraverted feeling type they make decisions and seek control of their environment through personal values. Unlike the extravert, they choose these values without reference to other people or society at large. They are perhaps the most naturally autonomous of the personality types (extraverted thinkers at their most stubborn still appear to be in submission to principles of reason).

Introverted feeling types are driven by an internal personal ideal. That ideal may take the form of a mystical or ecstatic vision. Where that ideal can be harnessed to external realities they make untiring workers: they look for work with a purpose rather than merely as a way of obtaining material goods.

Like the introverted thinkers they tend to live their lives largely with their auxiliary perceptive function. Thus they are open-minded and flexible (unless their ideal is threatened in some way).

Those whose auxiliary is sensing (ISFP) are the more realistic and may display great powers of concentration when tackling tasks requiring careful monitoring. They may express their feelings through concrete actions. People of this type, more than any other, have a tendency to play down their achievements.

Those who approach the external world through intuition (INFP) are likely to be the more insightful (even visionary). They also tend to be much more articulate than their sensing counterparts. In fact, they often show a marked literary tendency. According to Briggs Myers they may excel in any academic field which involves people-related possibilities.

Introverted sensation types (IS_J)

In this case sensation is dominant but introverted. But what can this possibly mean? Sensation refers to the five senses, surely they are irrevocably associated with external realities! This is true but only half of the story. There are two poles in every act of perception: the perceived object and the person doing the perceiving. For the extraverted sensing type the object is what matters. For the introvert what matters is his perception. Jung referred doubters to their local art gallery: two artists may express their perceptions of the same scene and produce two entirely different works of art (and today when art no longer has to be representational the visitor to the gallery may not even realise that the two paintings were evoked by the same scene).

If you like, the introverted senser gives depth to the sensation. Where the extravert is content with the objective details (the snapshot) the introvert must interpret it: 'We could say that introverted sensation transmits an image which does not so much reproduce the object as spread over it the patina of age-old subjective experience and the shimmer of events still unborn.'[8]

Jung proceeds to describe this type in almost entirely negative terms (perhaps because he encountered them mainly as cases in his consulting room). Briggs Myers saw them in a much more positive light, focussing on their dependability rather than the difficulty of understanding their approach to the senses.

This dependability arises from their respect for facts combined with a decisive responsible attitude to the external world.

To an outsider their interest in facts may seem prosaic: they expect you to express yourself clearly and factually. Only as you get to know them do you discover that they see these facts from a very individual perspective. Indeed they may have a great capacity for seeing the unexpected and the humorous in what, to most of us, is just the dull and the everyday.

They come across to outsiders as dependable not least because they approach the outside world through their auxiliary judging function, thinking or feeling. However, they are less likely to appear dominating than extraverted judging types. Thus they are more likely to create the impression of gracious efficiency which leads others to see them as dependable. We have a friend who is a good example of this type: every area of his life is characterised by efficiency and good planning. When he moved house recently he approached the choice of new schools for his children with military precision. The same precision even affects the way he plans holidays.

Their least developed function is intuition. Thus they are likely to be uncomfortable in situations where they cannot see the sense in what they have been asked to do (usually because an intuitive has left the working out!). However, they can be very tolerant: 'once they are convinced that a given thing does matter a lot to a given person, the need becomes a fact to be respected and they may go to generous lengths to help satisfy it, while still holding that it doesn't make sense.'[9]

Introverted intuitive types (IN_J)

The last of the eight groups tackled by Jung was those introverts for whom intuition is their dominant function. As with the introverted senser there is a question as to what it means to turn a mode of perception inwards. What Jung understood by it was a particular sensitivity to the entire realm of the

47

unconscious. These are the visionaries, seers and mystics. Jung comments that, 'Had this type not existed, there would have been no prophets in Israel.'[10] Alternatively, if they too easily allow their inner vision to shape their life, they may become the cranks and the false prophets of society.

Again what makes the difference between a crank and visionary is their possession of an adequately developed auxiliary function. Introverted intuitives will approach the external world decisively through their judging function, thinking or feeling. Thus they may be single-minded in the pursuit of their vision.

Unfortunately they may be single-minded in the pursuit of a *false* vision. Again their auxiliary function provides much needed balance here, enabling them to look critically at their cherished intuitions.

Those whose auxiliary is thinking will be more analytical. They also tend to be the most independent of the types. Their intuition gives them a ready supply of alternative possibilities and their thinking makes them naturally critical of the status quo.

Introverted intuitives whose auxiliary is feeling (INFJ) are much more person-oriented. However, underneath they are every bit as individualistic as their thinking counterparts.

Their blind spot may well be the world of sense perceptions. Indeed they may be so unaware of sensation that they neglect their own bodies. The image of the absent-minded professor who forgets to take regular meals, or sleep, or who may even neglect to dress properly is not so far-fetched.

Myers–Briggs and the Four Temperaments

The preceding descriptions are of value in helping people to become more aware of how the various attitudes and functions spotlighted by the Myers–Briggs Type Indicator interrelate. However, it is not always convenient to work through each of the sixteen types whenever we want to discuss how personality affects a particular aspect of life. Furthermore, although considerable work has been done on building up statistics relating to personality type, in many cases there is still insufficient data to justify such fine tuning. Thus it is both more convenient and realistic to look for less detailed combinations of preferences.

Probably the best-known of these approaches is that of David Keirsey and Marilyn Bates (popularised in their book *Please Understand Me*). They sought and found four combinations of preferences (SJ, SP, NT, NF) which roughly correlated with the four classical temperament types.

The Promethean temperament (NT)

This temperament is named after the mythological character who stole fire from the gods and brought technology to humankind.

People of this type are characterised above all by the will to power (perhaps more obvious in those for whom thinking rather than intuition is dominant): this need not be power over other people but may be (physical or intellectual) power over the environment. They are prototypical of the autonomous individual.

Particularly in its introverted forms, it resembles the melancholic type of classical psychology.

The Apollonian temperament (NF)

This type is regarded by Keirsey as motivated primarily by the quest for authenticity, for self-actualisation. He named it after the god Apollo, the god of culture and statecraft, the god of reason, but also the god of the kind of religious ecstasy the Greeks associated with self-fulfilment.

Such people are idealistic, romantic and empathetic. They may also be articulate and enthusiastic. As a result they may be extremely persuasive leaders. According to Oswald and Kroeger, they 'can be the most seductive of all types . . .

because they seduce themselves first'.[11] Interestingly a disproportionately high percentage of clergy appear to be NF.

Looking at the four classical temperaments the one which
comes closest to this type is the born agitator, the choleric.

The Epimethean temperament (SJ)

This type was (rather inappropriately) named after the obscure
brother of Prometheus who opened Pandora's Box and
unloosed upon the world all the evils which the gods had impri-
soned within. If Epimetheus really was an SJ then this story
was a slander put about by his NT brother for the chief characteristic of the SJ is a desire for stability.

SJs are the glue of human society because they work to
maintain the status quo; they are the natural conservatives.
Comparing this description with the classical temperaments the
one that it corresponds to most closely is the phlegmatic.

The Dionysian temperament (SP)

The last of the four temperament types is named after the
Greek god Dionysus (or Bacchus), the god of fertility, of wine,
of music, of poetry, of all that leads to ecstasy. This is the most
action-oriented of the temperaments. They are spontaneous,
impulsive, always craving experience. Amongst the classical
temperaments, the closest correspondence is with the sanguine
type.

THE FOUR 'QUADRANTS'

Another way of grouping the sixteen personality types is to
divide up the type table (see above) into its four quadrants (IS,
IN, ES, EN). In effect, this means focussing exclusively on the
interaction between extraversion/introversion and the perceiving functions. While this may sound arbitrary, those who use

the Myers–Briggs Type Indicator in education find this a particularly convenient grouping because of an observed correlation between academic achievement and these four types.

The thoughtful innovators (IN)

These are introverts with a preference for intuition (either as their dominant or auxiliary function). They may be expected to be introspective and to show a liking for theory, speculation, and complexity for their own sake. American statistical studies reveal a disproportionately high percentage of this type amongst those of high academic achievement.

The action-oriented innovators (EN)

These are extraverts with a preference for intuition. They show a similar interest in possibilities, patterns, and relationships to that of the preceding type but see them as opportunities to make things happen. Being extraverts they are likely to have a much wider range of interests than the INs. Again they tend to do well academically but are more likely to take that success as a launch-pad into the 'real world' than to stay within the ivory-tower of an academic environment.

The thoughtful realists (IS)

These are introverts who prefer sensing. This leads to a more down-to-earth, methodical, realistic outlook than that of the INs. Although such qualities are vital for many aspects of everyday life they are not usually associated with high academic achievement. They may be very successful at school simply by virtue of sheer hard work only to find that the expectations of university are very different.

The action-oriented realists (ES)

This type combines extraversion with sensing. They are the most practical of the types and learn best when useful applications are obvious. Thus they may excel at design subjects or languages (particularly if they have to use the language). However, their need for constant activity and sensory stimulus means that they are put off by the controlled and rather cerebral environment of traditional schools. Thus a disproportionate number fail to achieve the academic standards of which they are capable.

Exercises

(a) Helping Lisa

Lisa is a problem for her teachers. She's bright enough, but she seems to value popularity above everything else. Talkative, friendly and gregarious, she relies on her friends to make decisions for her and she patterns her behavior after theirs. Adults see her as flighty, unsure of her own preferences and point of view. Her work and conversations are often trite and shallow. Sometimes her classmates are annoyed by her 'helpfulness'; they wish she would mind her own business. When criticized by a teacher or her friends, she seems deeply hurt and resentful.[12]

Lisa clearly needs help to develop a mind of her own. Can type theory give us a place from which to start?

Begin by making an educated guess about her type. Is she extravert or introvert? Feeling or thinking? What does her over-zealous 'helpfulness' suggest to you about her preference for judging or perception? We are told little about her preference for sensing or intuition. Given that her work tends to be trite and shallow, which would you opt for?[13]

In the light of your guess, what would you expect her strengths and weaknesses to be? What positive suggestions would you make to her the next time she is rebuffed by a friend? Is she more likely to respond favourably to honest praise or to criticism?

(b) A marriage in crisis

A couple have come to you for advice. Beryl complains that Tom behaves as if she doesn't exist. Whatever she does fails to get a response. Neither tears nor outbursts of anger seem to move him. He never says he loves her, refuses to talk about his day at the office, and he seems completely self-contained. She recognises that he is a conscientious provider and a responsible parent to their children. However, she fears they are growing apart and his unresponsiveness leaves her feeling empty and depressed.

Tom listens quietly to Beryl's complaints. He agrees with her description of the facts. As far as he is concerned, he regards Beryl as a good wife and mother. He wants the marriage to continue, but he doesn't know what to do to make it happier.

Fortuitously Tom and Beryl have both taken the Myers–Briggs Type Indicator. He is an ISTJ and she an ESFJ. Assuming that they are both normal well-adjusted people, what advice would you give them?

What effect will their differences of preference have on their ability to communicate with each other? They share a preference for S and J. In what ways might this help them to communicate? In what ways might it exacerbate their problem?

In what ways might an understanding of type enable Beryl to take steps to improve communications? How might it help Tom? Bearing in mind their psychological types, what specific activities could you suggest that might help to rebuild their relationship?

N.B. If you would like to find out more about workshops based on the Myers–Briggs Type Indicator, we have included some useful addresses at the end of the book.

4

Personalities in Prayer

In this chapter we shall begin to examine the relevance of type theory for the Christian life. Christian prayer can take many different forms. To what extent does that variety arise from differences in temperament?

WHAT IS CHRISTIAN PRAYER?

Prayer or something very similar is at the heart of all religion. But are all the practices which are given the collective name of prayer legitimate for the Christian? For example, the term includes any technique for manipulating a god or some other supernatural being so as to achieve one's desires. This is clearly not Christian prayer. But can we be more specific about what constitutes Christian prayer?

A striking feature of biblical prayers is their conversational nature. From Abraham to Jesus the great pray-ers of the Bible appear to engage in conversation with God. The character of the conversation varies as much as do ordinary ones: an expression of admiration or awe; bargaining like the merchants in a Middle Eastern market-place; an angry protest; the intimacy of a child speaking to a beloved parent. But whatever its tone biblical prayer is always the expression of a personal relationship. It would be an exaggeration to say that this was true for all subsequent Christian traditions but it has certainly been an important feature of Christian (and Jewish) prayer for many centuries. In a word, it has the form of a dialogue.

Speaking of prayer in these terms reminds us that we are not just objects on which God acts redemptively. On the contrary, the overwhelming testimony of the Bible and the Judaeo-Christian traditions is that God always treats us with respect as persons and potential partners in the ushering in of the Kingdom.

Prayer as partnership

Since Christian prayer is a *dia*logue between the triune God and the believing individual (or community) it is shaped by both partners to the dialogue. Thus it is affected by the character of the God whom we worship; it is affected by our own personalities; and, particularly in the case of communal prayer, it is affected by the structures of the believing community to which we belong.

Traditionally, Christian spirituality has concentrated exclusively on the first of these factors: the character of the one to whom we pray. And that should not surprise us. The Bible makes it abundantly clear that God is the senior partner in prayer. Thus the divine character (the *theological* factor) is the common basis for *all* Christian prayer. This has several important implications for the nature of Christian prayer.

Since God is the senior partner in the relationship, our prayer is best thought of as a response: our response to what he has already done for us, is doing for us, and promises to do for us. In prayer we commit ourselves to following his actions and doing so on his conditions. One of the insights of traditional Roman Catholic spirituality is that when we pray we align our will with that of God.

However, there are forms of prayer which, although superficially similar to this aspect of Christian prayer, are in fact fundamentally at odds with the Christian faith. For example, Christian prayer is not resigned acceptance of the way the world is. Nor is it the contemplative adoration of the infinite advocated by some mystics. More generally, forms of spirituality which advocate our alignment with some impersonal cosmic force are quite inappropriate for Christians. They are inappropriate because they misrepresent the character of the God we claim to worship. Specifically they deny the personhood of God and may also have difficulty maintaining that God is both utterly transcendent and intimately present to every creature.

Similarly manipulative prayer is ruled out by the requirement that prayer be regarded as dialogue. By manipulative prayer, we mean any technique which is intended to enable the practitioner to achieve his or her own ends by manipulating the spiritual dimension of reality. This includes not only magical incantations but also positive thinking, and some forms of visualisation exercise.

Yet another approach that is ruled out by these considerations is the notion of prayer as a therapeutic device. This understanding of prayer may obscure the fact that Christian prayer is addressed to another. Such prayer may become a monologue; a form of self-expression; a way of getting in touch with unconscious aspects of your own personality.

We come back to the fact that prayer is a dialogue: an expression of a personal relationship. Indeed it expresses the most intimate relationship a human being can experience. Thus it is appropriate to include the whole of our life in prayer. This means that the content of prayer is incredibly diverse.

However, if we rest content with the theological dimension of prayer we fail to do it justice. We will stress the unity of prayer at the expense of its diversity. This may result in us ascribing all differences in the way Christians pray to theological differences. And it may cause us to despise or condemn those who pray differently. Hence one benefit of type theory is that it makes us more conscious of the variety that is possible within Christian prayer.

The place of technique

Many Christians have been helped by prayer techniques. These range from simple frameworks for a prayer time (e.g., *A*dor-ation, *C*onfession, *T*hanksgiving, *S*upplication) to detailed instructions or set prayers for the entire year.

Other Christians question the legitimacy of set prayers and formal structures in what is essentially a personal relationship. If they permit set prayers at all it is only 'because man in his weakness, desires a crutch in his relationship with the divine.'[1] And the more unbending will be tempted to condemn the use of set prayers as quenching the Spirit. In reality, of course, many of those who decry ritual and formality in prayer unwit-tingly reintroduce it in other ways. We all know people who when they pray 'spontaneously' rely heavily on stock phrases ('Dear loving heavenly Father . . .') or use 'Jesus' as a sort of holy punctuation mark.

It may be useful to compare such structures in prayer with the rituals of everyday life. We all have rituals with which we structure our day and our personal relationships. Couples often use stock ways of expressing their affection or ritualised forms of address (just look at the range of pet names in the personal columns of *The Times* next St Valentine's Day).

Significantly our attitude to such everyday rituals is strongly affected by our temperament. As we have seen, people who deal with the external world primarily through their judging function (whether thinking or feeling) are more likely to want to structure their world. And, if this is combined with a prefer-ence for sensing perception, such people may well be inclined to perpetuate lots of little rituals (e.g., demanding that dinner be served precisely on the last stroke of six o'clock). Other personality types find that such rituals simply bore or irritate them.

Such rituals are helpful when they help us to live our lives more effectively. Indeed creative artists often devise rituals to enable them to get down to work. The novelist may insist on writing with a particular kind of pencil and he may ritually sharpen twenty of these pencils before beginning work. In the case of Stravinsky, his work-room was laid out with the precision of an operating theatre, the very act of composition was ritualised, and the musical scores he wrote have been described as inhumanly meticulous.

The real danger in technique lies not in its formalism but in the risk of obsession. There is a fine line between the successful composer with his elaborate ritual and the failure who never succeeds in achieving the standards he sets in his rituals.

In prayer there is a similar danger. We can become so obsessed with prayer techniques and approaches to spirituality that we lose sight of the point of prayer. Technique can hinder our relationship with God. In some cases it may even be a covert way of protecting ourselves from the demands God makes on us.

THE PSYCHOLOGICAL FUNCTIONS AND OUR PRAYER PREFERENCES

Sensing and prayer

We have already seen that sensing types perceive reality primarily through the five senses. They are down-to-earth, practical, and emphasise the present moment. But what forms of prayer and spirituality correspond most closely to this form of perception?

As far as using the Bible is concerned, sensing is likely to encourage a 'commonsense' approach. A passage will be taken verse by verse or word by word and read for its literal, practical sense. Indeed it may be read in minute detail. A person who likes to approach Scripture in this way may exhibit a preference for the more concrete, practical passages. Such a person may revel in the Gospel stories (particularly those of St Mark) while paying less attention to the more abstract theology of St Paul's letters.

Sensing prayer may be characterised by its simplicity and directness. The spiritual is something to be seen, touched, and felt. God is experienced as simple presence. It calls for us to experience God in the present moment through our five senses.

Many of the techniques for relaxing and stilling oneself in the presence of God may be regarded as forms of sensing prayer. Thus, for example, prayerfully becoming aware of my bodily sensations, the feel of the clothes clinging to my body or the sensation of air passing in and out of my lungs, is a form of sensing prayer; the point being to become aware of the God who is closer to me than my own body. Similarly hearing, sight, and even taste and smell can become vehicles of prayer.

One classical form of sensing prayer is the so-called *prayer of simple regard*. This is a wordless, image-less being in the presence of God. It is just being present. If you like, it is a sensing of the silence and through that of the presence of God. This may sound very different from the notion of Christian prayer as dialogue. It is true that without words there can be no dialogue. Thus spoken prayer must remain the primary form of Christian prayer. But it is equally true that silence has a legitimate (even necessary) place in every personal relationship. The prayer of simple regard may be seen as the prayer analogue of those occasions in every human relationship when speech is not necessary or desirable: when the one thing needful is to hold the hand of your beloved. There may well be times when words cannot express your sorrow or comfort your pain. In such circumstances you can always take God's hand, as it were, and simply shelter in the presence of your divine lover.

However, the most familiar form of sensing prayer is more active than this sensing of God through silence, focussing instead on listening and speaking. It may be straightforward down-to-earth conversational prayer. Or it may take the form of entering the presence of God via the recitation of psalms, saying the rosary, or repeating the Jesus Prayer.

In the Protestant tradition a proper concern for the word is sometimes translated into an exclusive concentration on speaking and hearing. Perhaps that is why our places of worship are sometimes so ugly. For example, we know of a recently constructed church which could be a lecture theatre rather than a place of worship (in fact it has to be lit by artificial light even on a sunny day). Other Christian traditions have made more of the sense of sight. Romanesque and Gothic cathedrals were designed not merely to keep their congregations dry during services. They were designed to inspire and guide our prayer and worship.

Another way in which some Christians use seeing in prayer is through the contemplation of icons. This is often misunderstood by Protestants as a form of idolatry. But icons were never intended as objects of worship. Nor were they intended to stimulate our imaginations or evoke pious feelings. In a helpful introduction to this form of prayer, Henri Nouwen comments that 'Icons are painted to lead us into the inner room of prayer and bring us close to the heart of God.'[2] And they lead us into prayer by engaging the sense of sight.

Another characteristic of sensing spirituality is its emphasis on the present. There is a tendency for the person who likes to use this approach to accept the status quo: the details I observe, the institutions I experience just *are* and I have to accept them and live with them. Such a person will set great store by tradition. The danger, of course, is that a proper valuation of tradition may give way to arid traditional*ism*.

Intuition and prayer

Just as there is a sharp difference between perception through the senses and through intuition, so there is a distinction in the corresponding approaches to prayer and spirituality. Where sensing focusses on the details of present reality, intuition concentrates on patterns, possibilities, and the future.

The intuitive approach to the Bible is likely to be much

freer in the use of imagination than the sensing approach. An intuitive reading of a Bible passage is unlikely to focus on each word in succession. On the contrary it may neglect the individual words in the interest of the overall meaning. The comparison with intuitive reading of secular literature may be instructive: the individual words merely serve to evoke the story, to create and populate a world within the imagination.

This does not mean that sensing people are unimaginative. Rather they use their imaginations in a different way. Someone for whom the five senses are important is likely to use imagination to evoke the sensual details of a scene. For example, in imagining the feeding of the five thousand they may be able to imagine the feel of the ground beneath their feet, the hot Mediterranean sun on their face, the texture of the bread, and the taste of the fish. The intuitive may evoke the overall feel of the crowd and the possibilities inherent in the situation (they may also be more likely to go beyond the written word and speculate about alternative histories).

Precisely the same thing goes on in the Ignatian contemplations. Apparently the young Ignatius stumbled on the imaginative approach to Scripture when, during a long illness, he was reduced to reading the Bible and the Lives of the Saints. He found that the method he customarily used with secular literature worked admirably. His *Spiritual Exercises* is largely a careful elaboration of the imaginative approach of placing oneself in the story and reliving it. For those who are suspicious of a prayer technique so closely associated with Roman Catholicism, it is worth noting that the great Puritan theologian Richard Baxter adopted a similar technique in his devotional classic *The Saints' Everlasting Rest*.

The intuitive approach, being less focussed on the words, is also likely to be less literal. Symbolism is of more interest because of its capacity to evoke images for the mind's eye. It is often suggested that the rich imagery of John's Gospel, the Book of Revelation, and the Old Testament prophets makes them particularly accessible to the intuitive approach.

Similarly intuitive prayer may rely heavily on imagination and fantasy. Such an approach may use symbols and images rather than words to communicate with God. For example, instead of asking God to heal Adrian's migraine in so many words, the intuitive may imagine Jesus entering the darkened room in which the sufferer is lying and laying healing hands upon his head.

There is another form of intuitive prayer which at first sight is so different to this free use of images as to seem quite incompatible with it. In this form the presence of God is intuited in silence and stillness. This is superficially similar to the prayer of present regard. However, there is a significant difference which one American theologian has summed up as follows:

> The difference consists in the focused or unfocused character of the gaze. To use a playful distinction . . . in the prayer of simple regard we are *now/here*, fully present to the present actuality of life, whereas in what I call the prayer of the vacant stare we are *no/where* (recall that the Greek term for nowhere is *Utopia*).[3]

Because intuition focusses on possibilities rather than concrete realities, it is future oriented. In religious terms its keyword is *hope*. Thus, unlike sensing types, intuitives tend to value novelty and change above the security of tradition. Thus intuitives may be impatient with set prayers, traditional liturgies, etc. The danger, of course, is that they may seek novelty for its own sake (what C. S. Lewis called 'the liturgical fidget'). Their prayer and hence their relationship with God may become mercurial, inconsistent, and erratic.

Interestingly journal keeping is often recommended as a spiritual discipline for intuitives. Lawrence finds it helpful not so much because it enables him to express his intuitive insights but rather because it forces him to put them into words and thus ground them in reality.

Thinking and prayer

Thinking has been so badly neglected as a dimension of prayer and spirituality that we are likely to be surprised when prayer is described as thinking.[4] More common would be the following comment from a distinguished Roman Catholic spiritual writer: 'prayer is to be made less with the head than with the heart. In fact, the sooner it gets away from the head and from thinking the more enjoyable and the more profitable it is likely to become. Most priests and religious equate prayer with thinking. That is their downfall.'[5]

As we explained in Chapter 2, the thinking function is one of the two functions by which we make decisions and organise our world. It is responsible for those decisions which are arrived at by means of logic and objective considerations.

The thinking function comes to the fore in an intellectual approach to Scripture. Thus a thinking type may approach a book of the Bible carefully and systematically, perhaps with the help of one or more commentaries. He may take weeks over it, seeking a deeper understanding of God's word, analysing the structure of the book, learning about its cultural context, establishing the precise meanings of terms in the book, etc.

To someone who values thinking, truth is of crucial importance. Indeed he or she may have become a Christian because, in the light of the available evidence, Christianity seemed the most rational way of understanding the world. As my comments on the 'thinker's' approach to Scripture suggest, such a person is likely to understand the spiritual life at least partly in terms of a search for truth and meaning. Feeding the mind in the study of the Bible or theology is thus inextricably bound up with prayer. And a moment of intellectual insight is likely to be regarded by them as a high point of prayer.

Again this has parallels in the realm of personal relationships between humans. In one of her books, Anne Townsend recounts the case of an engineering student who would express his affection for his girlfriend by sharing his engineering textbooks with her! It may not be everyone's cup of tea but, for 'thinkers' at least, the cut and thrust of intellectual discussion is an essential part of a personal relationship.

It is customary today to draw a distinction between prayer and study. For example, the headings suggested by the Third Order of the Society of St Francis for a tertiary's rule of life include prayer, spiritual reading, and study. My own experience (as a thinking type) is that study and spiritual reading are impossible to disentangle. And both frequently shade imperceptibly into prayer.

Unfortunately for 'thinkers' the Church today (particularly where it is charismatic) is dominated by 'feelers'. Their reaction when a thinking type shares an insight with them is often uncomprehending or dismissive. We are told to stop using our heads and start using our hearts. One spiritual director with much experience of handling thinking types makes this comment about such a reaction:

> I wish to assert in the strongest possible terms . . . that this should *never* be said to the thinker about prayer, unless by someone with whom there is a long relationship of mutual trust and confidence and the assurance that the directee is able to supply a context for the remark. Outside such a context, saying this is equivalent to saying: 'Your experience of God is not valid.'[6]

The 'thinker' reminds the church that knowing God is every bit as important as loving God. And in these days of charismatic renewal an objective rational judgement is an invaluable aid to discerning the spirits.

As with the other psychological functions, however, there are dangers in putting too much emphasis on the role of thinking in prayer. Much of the anti-intellectualism in the Church today is a very natural reaction to past overemphasis on thinking. The tendency of 'thinkers' to share on an intellectual level easily degenerates into an intellectual élitism. Where thinking is overvalued mere erudition may be confused with spiritual maturity, and genuinely holy men and women may be overlooked or despised because they cannot read Greek and Hebrew.

Feeling and prayer

The feeling function enables us to make decisions and organise our world on the basis of personal considerations and value judgements (aesthetic, moral, etc.). Its effect in the spiritual life is an emphasis on relationships, intimacy, and affection.

In Bible study the personal application will be very important. An element of warmth is essential. A person who reads the Bible with this function to the fore may well describe it as God's love letter: it will be seen as a very intimate work directed personally at him or her.

Feeling spirituality apprehends God with the heart. Thus in contrast to the desire for insight associated with thinking this approach seeks the affective moment: the experience of being beloved by God. Some of the ecstatic experiences associated with the charismatic renewal may be in tune with the feeling approach.

In public worship, the feeling function is catered for more by the Eucharist than the sermon. Communion may be regarded as a time of particular intimacy with God. But for feeling types public worship is also important because of the aspect of being part of a worshipping community.

People who are naturally oriented towards the feeling function often have better developed social skills than thinking types. They are people-oriented, concerned for the needs and feelings of the other person. For that reason their prayer may well be dominated by intercessions.

We have already cited the Ignatian exercises as a good example of intuitive prayer. However, they may equally well be seen as a prime example of feeling prayer. This is because the intuitive contemplation often leads to a feeling-oriented imaginative dialogue.

Journal keeping, while perhaps not naturally associated with people whose feeling function is well developed, may be a good way for others to develop their feeling. Many journal exercises are designed specifically to help with the expression of feelings and to become more aware of our personal relationships.

This dimension has never been lacking in evangelical spirituality: Pietism, Methodism, the Holiness Movement, Pentecostalism, and, most recently, the Charismatic Movement have all regarded feeling as important. However, as with the other functions it can be dangerous to overemphasise feeling. The danger is simply that we concentrate on feeling (and experience) at the expense of truth. This may be expressed as a sort of spiritual pragmatism which regards every spiritual discipline which makes you feel good as a legitimate part of Christian spirituality.

THE JUNGIAN ATTITUDES AND PRAYER

Prayer and the extravert

Extraversion is an orientation towards the external world. Its counterpart in spirituality is a tendency to look for God in the world. God is seen to be at work in the world and this may evoke a response in terms of practical service.

For the extravert the voice of God may be more readily discerned through the natural world, current events, and other people. Thus sermons, especially those with a prophetic quality, may be particularly important: the words of the preacher are to be understood as the words of God. One of the pioneers of the charismatic renewal once advised Diana that provided you listened with the ears of faith even a poor sermon could become God's message to you.

Conversely a temperament which is oriented towards the external world may have difficulty coping with silence in worship. Lively prayer meetings, audible communal worship, activity in prayer are the order of the day.

Prayer and the introvert

Introversion denotes an inward orientation. In keeping with this, an introverted style of spirituality will seek God within. Thus one of the greatest western theologians could record that 'Under your guidance I entered into the depths of my soul.'[7]

Thus the journey to God is interpreted as a journey inwards. God is more easily discerned speaking from within through the voice of conscience or the private reading of Scripture.

Naturally such an orientation is likely to lead to an emphasis on silence, reflection, and private prayer. In extreme cases it may result in an aversion to public worship. More common but by no means universal amongst introverts may be a degree of difficulty in expressing one's spiritual experience.

Prayer and perception

The person who relates to the external world through his perceiving function (whether sensing or intuition) will tend to emphasise awareness and experience rather than control. Such people are naturally spontaneous.

The effect on prayer and spirituality is likely to be a corresponding spontaneity. Free prayer and unstructured worship are likely to be preferred to a more formal liturgical approach to worship. Similarly on a personal level such people may well be impatient with a carefully structured quiet time.

The potential for mutual misunderstanding is considerable. Other Christians may be tempted to dismiss the perceiving person as undisciplined or, worse, unspiritual because of his apparent inability to maintain a structured programme of prayer and Bible study. Conversely, the perceiving person may dismiss those other Christians as formalistic, regarding their structures as a way in which they quench the Spirit.

Prayer and judging

The judging person uses his or her judging function (thinking or feeling) to relate to the external world. This results in an orientation towards order and control.

Such people are likely to approach the Bible in a disciplined and orderly fashion. Robert Murray M'Cheyne's plan for reading the entire Bible in a year is a good example of a Bible reading scheme by a judging person for other people with the same orientation.

Similarly they thrive on long-term planning in prayer. Such people are naturally attracted to detailed prayer and meditation programmes such as Mark Link's *You*, Una Kroll's *The Spiritual Exercise Book* and the five volume *Take and Receive* series.

PUTTING IT ALL TOGETHER

It is one thing to discuss the effect of the individual psychological functions and attitudes on prayer; it is quite another to consider the impact of the interplay of functions which take place in every human being. As you will already have gathered, this can be very complex.

One temptation to which users of Jungian type theory are prone is to attempt to correlate psychological types with particular ways of praying or schools of spirituality. The most widely used classification of this sort is one suggested by Michael and Norrissey.[8] They keep the system manageable by correlating the four temperament types of Keirsey and Bates with four major schools of Roman Catholic spirituality. Thus SJ correlates with *Ignatian* spirituality; SP with *Franciscan* spirituality; NT with *Thomistic* spirituality; and NF with *Augustinian* spirituality. A similar correlation is offered by Charles Keating.[9]

Keating is careful to warn against the danger of turning these correlations into stereotypes and, having made them, devotes much of the rest of his book to stressing the rich diversity of individual human personalities. Too much emphasis on such correlations encourages us to attempt to slot into a particular prayer tradition which, although it may correlate with our personality type, is actually inappropriate for our particular circumstances.

A variety of factors besides our personality type are important in determining the prayer approach to which we are likely to be attracted. In the article referred to earlier, Thomas Clarke mentions two: the fact that prayer is usually a leisure time activity; and the influence of personal development on prayer style.

Jungian analysis suggests that when we relax we tend to exercise our less preferred psychological functions. If, as Clarke proposes, prayer ought to be regarded as a leisure activity, then our preferred style of prayer may not correspond exactly with our personality type.

A further complicating factor is that we do not stand still as human beings. Personal growth is a fact of human life and this applies also to our use of the four psychological functions. According to type theory, normal human development includes an increasing facility in each of the four functions. Over a period of years it should be possible to trace a gradual improvement in our use of our less preferred functions. Any approach to prayer which tries to put us in a pigeonhole is running counter to this development. What is appropriate for us now may not be helpful in ten years' time.

That brings us to the other danger of making too close a correlation between personality types and schools of spirituality. Such an approach invariably oversimplifies the traditions it selects in order to make them fit the typology better. Thus we may miss a potentially valuable approach to prayer because it has been classified as inappropriate for people of our type.

If you think about it, it is inherently unlikely that the great prayer traditions of the Christian Church are very closely linked to personality type. The reason is simply that, until relatively recently, personal preference was not a significant factor in deciding what tradition you belonged to. Thus the traditions which have thrived for centuries have done so precisely because they were capable of accommodating people of widely differing personality types.

A good example is the Franciscan tradition (which Michael and Norrissey associate with the SP temperament). Francis himself was such an incredible eccentric that it is hard to determine his type (possibly ESFP). But the first great theologian of the Franciscan order (and one of the seminal spiritual writers of the Middle Ages), St Bonaventure, was unmistakably NT. And a later Franciscan, St Peter of Alcantara, produced a volume of spiritual exercises to rival those of St Ignatius!

An example of more direct relevance to evangelicals is Michael and Norrissey's Augustinian type (NF). This has also been described as the evangelical type of spirituality. But such a description is seriously misleading. Looked at from within, evangelicalism is quite diverse. Arguably it is a loose coalition of spiritual and theological traditions united mainly by a common emphasis on the Bible and a desire to share its good news with those who have not heard.

As one unravels the various strands which go to make up modern evangelicalism one finds traditions which give pride of place to each one of the psychological functions. Feeling has often played an important part in evangelical Christianity (nowhere more so than in its pietist and charismatic varieties). But thinking too has been taken seriously particularly amongst the Puritans and Calvinists.

Similarly the sensing function may find satisfaction within evangelical Christianity. Remember that it was the churches of the Reformation that set up the cry *sola scriptura*. For the sensing evangelical it is the *hearing* of the Word that is central.

Evangelicalism has been more ambivalent about intuition than any of the other functions. Certainly today imagination and fantasy are dirty words in some evangelical circles. But intuitives have not been lacking within the tradition. We have already mentioned Richard Baxter. Another example might be John Bunyan whose *Pilgrim's Progress* is a classic case of imagination harnessed in the service of the gospel.

Exercises

To conclude the chapter, here are four prayer exercises focussing on each of the psychological functions in turn.

(a) Sensing prayer

A prayerful walk in which you consciously exercise several of your senses is a good example of sensing prayer. This version was written with a walk in a park or the countryside in mind. However, it could easily be adapted for use in an urban environment.

(1) Since it is a time of prayer, begin by taking a few moments to relax and become aware of God's loving presence.

(2) As you step outside, breathe deeply . . . reflect on how you take the air you breathe for granted. Consider the other necessities of life which God provides. Give thanks for that provision.

(3) *Sight*: Use your vision to revel in, enjoy, discern the colour, shape, texture, depth, movement of everything around you. Think about what the beauty in all around you contributes to your life. Consider the privilege and responsibility which God has given you in the gift of all this beauty. Express to God your thanksgiving and praise.

(4) *Hearing*: Stop for a while and really listen, listen to the silence which, in reality, is teeming with natural sounds. Listen for the breeze blowing through the trees or through the long grass; listen for the song of birds, and for the hum of insects. Imagine the wind, the trees, the insects, and the

birds all blending their voices together in a song of praise to their Creator. Add your voice to their worship.

(5) *Touch*: Become conscious of the feeling of the sun and the air on your skin, the textures of clothing, trees, grass, stones, the sensation of the ground through your shoes.

(6) If you have time, you might like to do the same with your senses of taste and smell.

(7) As you revel in the sensations of creation, recall that all this is God's work of art. And God is creatively present in everything around you. Allow yourself to become aware of that presence.

(b) Intuitive prayer

This example of intuitive prayer is an Ignatian exercise based on the story of Jesus' temptation in the wilderness (Matt. 4:1–11).

(1) Begin by relaxing; seeking inner and outer peace. Ask the Holy Spirit to lead you as you explore your personal wilderness; and ask Jesus to be with you and lend you his strength in your explorations.

(2) Read the passage several times slowly and reflectively. Note any particularly striking words or phrases.

(3) Imagine that you are following Jesus into the wilderness. Build up a mental image of the surroundings in which you find yourself. What does your wilderness look like? Is it a desert, or a dark forest, or a frozen tundra, or an empty house, or . . . ?

Examine your feelings about this wilderness. Become aware of that which is most oppressive, most fearful, threatening, confusing, tempting in your experience.

Now, become aware that Jesus is with you. Tell him about your fears and temptations, and the feelings associated with them. This could become the basis for an imaginative dialogue: wait in an attitude of openness for Jesus' response; address him again in the light of that response; and so on.

73

(4) Conclude by reflecting on the situation you have imagined. Does anything in particular strike you? How have these temptations affected your relationship with God? with others? In what ways can Jesus' strength to overcome temptations help you fulfil your ministry more effectively?

(c) Thinking prayer

'The Lord God took the man and put him in the garden of Eden to till it and keep it' (Gen. 2:15).

> We possess the things which God has committed to our hands, on the condition, that being content with a frugal and moderate use of them, we should take care of what shall remain. Let him who possesses a field, so partake of its yearly fruits, that he may not suffer the ground to be injured by his own negligence; but let him endeavour to hand it down to posterity as he received it, or even better cultivated. Let him so feed on its fruits, that he neither dissipates it by luxury, nor permits it to be marred or ruined by neglect. Moreover, that this economy, and this diligence, with respect to those good things which God has given us to enjoy, may flourish among us; let every one regard himself as the steward of God in all things which he possesses. Then he will neither conduct himself dissolutely, nor corrupt by abuse those things which God requires to be preserved.[10]

(1) Spend a few minutes quietening yourself, preparing for prayer and study.
(2) When you are ready, use the passages above as the basis for brainstorming, i.e., as you reread them note down whatever comes to mind, any thoughts and reactions. Don't try to censor them. They may seem completely irrelevant to the passages but note them down anyway.
(3) Go through your list and pick out one idea which seems particularly striking, interesting, or important.
(4) Turn this idea over in your mind. Think about its impli-

cations. Does it offer any insight into God? into his relationship with the world? into his relationship with us? into our relationship with the world?

(5) What are its practical implications? How should this idea affect my behaviour?

(6) Share your reflections with God and wait in silence for further insights.

(d) Feeling prayer

This exercise is an Ignatian exercise based on the Wedding at Cana (John 2:1–12). We have given it as an example of feeling prayer because of its emphasis on the feelings and relationships in the story.

(1) Spend a few minutes becoming quiet before God, letting yourself become open to his presence.

(2) Read the passage slowly and reflectively, letting yourself be particularly aware of the story and the images. Build up a mental picture of the scene at this wedding.

Imagine the bridal couple; picture them enjoying the company of their friends, sharing their joy. Experience the atmosphere of celebration; the joy, excitement, and laughter.

Place yourself in the scene. Perhaps you are one of the servants, or a guest.

You become aware that the wine is running out. Share in the anxiety that spreads amongst those who are conscious of the shortage. You see Mary approach Jesus, and listen to their exchange.

Now you watch (or take part in) what follows. Note your own feelings as the jars are filled with water, a sample is taken to the master of ceremonies, and he declares it to be the best wine.

What are your feelings about witnessing this manifestation of Jesus' power?

(3) You become aware that Jesus is standing before you; look-

ing at you. What do you see in his eyes? What are your feelings about this confrontation? Share your reaction with him. How does he respond? Use this as the basis for imaginative dialogue.

Communication and the Good News

What Is the Good News?

At the heart of the Christian religion lies a message of good news. However, the New Testament maintains a curious ambiguity about this message. This is demonstrated by the opening verse of Mark's Gospel: 'The beginning of the gospel of Jesus Christ.' It is not clear whether he means the good news proclaimed *by* Jesus Christ or the good news proclaimed *about* him. In practical terms this ambiguity need not detain us; after all the teaching of Jesus is an integral part of the proclamation *about* him.

But proclamation *about* Jesus is not as straightforward as we might at first imagine. Does it refer to the Bible's message, the Church's message, or our own personal message? Or are all three an integral part of what it means to proclaim the good news today? Clearly a satisfactory theoretical answer to these questions must be a theological one. However, our psychological preferences may be a significant factor in predisposing us to one theological answer rather than another.

In one sense the content of the good news can be summarised very simply in a telling of events. This man, Jesus, was born at a particular time and in a particular place (of a virgin mother). He became an itinerant preacher and healer, proclaiming a message of the imminence of God's Kingdom and the possibility of salvation. Eventually he was executed as a subversive and blasphemer. Three days later he was raised from the dead and the total event of his death and resurrection somehow gave effect to his message.

The Christian message is good news of salvation . . . from sin. But once again we run into that lack of definition we have already noticed. What is sin? The Bible defines it in theological terms as rebellion against God but, at least in the New Testament, it shies away from attempts to give too detailed an account of it in legal terms. Why is this? The New Testament is unequivocal that all humankind is in rebellion against God. But precisely because of this the forms and expressions of sin are manifold. No precise definition is capable of encompassing all the possible expressions. True, there are moral absolutes which are more or less universally recognised (e.g., theft and murder, while they may be understood differently in different cultures, are generally frowned upon). But other expressions of sin have taken longer to be recognised as such. Various forms of exploitation have taken centuries to be recognised as sinful (e.g., racism, the institution of slavery, sexism, child labour, drug dealing).

As we have already noted, each psychological type is likely to have its own preferred expression of sin. We need to remember that the gospel is addressed to a person with a specific set of needs and temptations.

If we are saved *from* sin we are also saved *for* something: for the Kingdom of God. The Shorter Catechism of the Westminster Assembly began with the question, 'What is the chief end of man?' to which it gave the answer, 'Man's chief end is to glorify God, and to enjoy him for ever.' That is as good a summary as any of what it means to be saved for the Kingdom of God.

The process of salvation to which Christ gave effect is a vocation: we are called to abandon our rebelliousness and to find new purpose in worshipping and glorifying God. Salvation is not primarily about self-fulfilment but rather about the unselfconsciousness of praise: the sort of attitude which has permitted Christian martyrs throughout the centuries to die praising God.

That ultimate vocation of praise must be the determining factor in how we understand our mission as Christians in the world. We are called to praise God and we are sent to increase the giving of glory to God within his creation. This means returning all reality to God with praise and thanksgiving so that all may be 'taken up into the spiral of mutual appreciation and delight which is the fulfilment of creation.'[1] But, in relation to our fellow human beings, this can only be done in a way that respects their freedom: we may encourage them to glorify God on their own behalf only by the proclamation of the good news (in the context of a personal relationship with God).

Ultimately this is what evangelism is about: it is offering to those around us the invitation to join with us in the cosmic hymn of praise to God our creator and our redeemer.

BECOMING ALL THINGS TO ALL MEN AND WOMEN

One of the features which makes our proclamation of Jesus Christ *good* news is the fact that it is addressed to all people. It is relevant to men and women of all cultures, races and socio-economic groups. It is also relevant to all psychological types.

The gospel is not a cultural package

We start here because considerable work has been done on the importance of cross-cultural communication for evangelism. By looking at this, we may learn things relevant to the issue of 'trans-temperamental' communication of the gospel!

The first intimations that the gospel was greater than any particular culture appear in Acts 10. Peter is summoned from Joppa to Caesarea to proclaim the good news to a Gentile. The Holy Spirit interrupts the proceedings and Cornelius and his household become Christians *without becoming Jews*. The first great controversy of the early Christian Church was on just this issue: was it necessary for Gentile converts to observe Jewish rituals and customs, to throw over Graeco-Roman culture in favour of Hellenistic Jewish culture? And the conclusion which the Church came to was that Christianity was not so bound up with Judaism that this was necessary.

More positively, Acts 17 presents us with an impression of Paul preaching to the Gentiles of Athens. The striking feature of his speech is the extent to which he is prepared to accommodate to Hellenistic categories of thought in order to communicate his message. He had clearly given some thought to where he might find points of entry into the culture.

Some Christians argue that Paul went too far in accommodating the gospel to Greek thought; that the opening chapters of 1 Corinthians represent a radical shift of emphasis in his preaching. They suggest that dialogue proved to be inadequate and so he returned to confrontation. It is certainly true that the Mars Hill speech emphasises dialogue while 1 Corinthians 1 and 2 emphasise confrontation. But closer examination of the texts reveals that both elements are present in both places. There was dialogue *and* confrontation.

Lest there be any doubt, a later passage in 1 Corinthians highlights the extent to which he was prepared to go in order to gain a sympathetic hearing for the gospel:

For though I am free from all men, I have made myself a slave to all, that I might win the more. To the Jews I became as a Jew, in order to win Jews; to those under the law I became as one under the law – though not myself being under the law – that I might win those under the law. To those outside the law I became as one outside the law – not being without law toward God but under the law of Christ – that I might win those outside the law. To the weak I became weak, that I might win the weak. I have become all things to all men, that I might by all means save some. I do

it all for the sake of the gospel, that I may share in its
blessings.   (1 Cor. 9:19–23)

What does this mean for the communication of the gospel in
other cultures? It suggests that the gospel can and must be
translated into different cultural contexts: that Christianity is
at home in every culture. We can find ways of expressing it in
every human culture. This may lead to expressions that seem
strange to western ears, e.g., the tribe in Irian Jaya for whom
Jesus is 'the sweet potato of life'. It certainly results in churches
whose practices seem quite alien to European or American
Christians. Every culture is capable of bearing an indigenous
expression of the gospel.

On the other hand, it would be equally true to say that
Christianity is at home in no human culture. Contrary to the
views of some Christians, Christianity is not Jewish. The Holy
Spirit made that clear at Caesarea. Neither is it Greek or Italian
or British or American. The identification of the gospel with
any one culture is a betrayal of the gospel comparable with the
betrayal perpetrated by the Judaisers within the New Testament church.

This has clear implications for cross-cultural evangelism (and
for evangelism which crosses the sub-cultures within our own
society).

To begin with, genuine Christian evangelism is not the same
thing as cultural imperialism. Cultural imperialism is precisely
what the Judaisers were about. Sadly, in spite of Paul's initial
victory over cultural imperialism, it has been the besetting sin
of both Protestant and Catholic missionary efforts. The film,
The Mission, displayed very graphically the effects of cultural
imperialism. Granted the thesis of the film, that the Jesuit
missionaries were indeed motivated by their faith to defend
the Amerindians against Spanish and Portuguese attempts to
enslave them, their own missionary efforts were still a form of
enslavement. The missionaries destroyed the culture of the
Amerindians in order to replace it with what they understood

as Christian culture. A similar process is taking place today whenever well-meaning Christians tell new converts that they can no longer listen to rock music because all such music is inherently evil.

On the contrary, for genuine Christian evangelism to take place the gospel must be spoken into the culture. Within the history of Protestant missions one of the most striking examples must surely be that of Hudson Taylor, the founder of the China Inland Mission (latterly known as the Overseas Missionary Fellowship). Within a few months of his arrival in China in 1855 he began to realise the need for complete identification with the people to whom he was ministering. The outward symbol of that identification was his adoption of Chinese dress (outrageous behaviour for a Victorian gentleman no matter how far he might be from London). It earned him the contempt of the expatriate community and the disapproval of his fellow missionaries but it also earned him a hearing amongst the Chinese people that no previous British missionary had achieved.

When we behave like Hudson Taylor we imply that all human culture is in some sense God-given. We recognise that God-givenness by giving the culture a fair hearing, attempting to understand it on its own terms, and looking for elements within it which may act as entry points for the gospel.

But speaking into the culture should not be confused with modifying the gospel for the sake of relevance or public acceptance. Dialogue need not degenerate into compromise. It has been defined as confrontation in love. This reflects the New Testament call to speak the truth in love. What this means for evangelism is that we will take the trouble to understand the person to whom we are speaking: we will want to know how they think, what they believe, what concerns them.

The gospel is not a psychological package

Christianity has made great strides in its understanding and respect for other cultures. However, it sometimes seems that less effort has been put into recognising and respecting the differences which make us distinct persons.

There is a temptation to generalise. For example, the impression is sometimes given that all we need to know for successful evangelism is that 'all have sinned and fall short of the glory of God' (Rom. 3:23). Now it is certainly true that without that element of confrontation the good news is unlikely to make much of an impact. However, as we have already pointed out the forms of sin are manifold: confrontation is much more likely to be effective if it is precisely targetted. And targetting a particular person's hang-ups, or fears, or prejudices, or superstitions is likely to be counter-productive unless you have already established a relationship of trust and understanding.

If the gospel is really for all men and women then it can speak to all temperaments. However, all too often the churches appear to contradict this view. Membership of a particular church appears to bring with it the expectation that we will adhere to certain patterns of worship and behaviour. It may take a cultural form: 'real Christianity expresses itself through the use of the Latin mass/Tudor church music/the unaccompanied chanting of the Psalms in Gaelic/Moody and Sankey hymns.' However, it can also take a psychological form: 'real Christians should be capable of sitting in complete silence for thirty minutes/walking into a pub and telling strangers about Jesus/planning their prayer lives with military precision.' All too often we set unwritten membership requirements which exclude those who differ from us in cultural background or temperament. In doing so we have set ourselves on the path which transforms the church from a divinely instituted community to a purely human institution. Is this why the Church of England makes so little headway outside its usual white middle-class constituency? Is this why Black Pentecostal churches remain predominantly black?

One of the helpful features of the Myers–Briggs Type Indicator is the extensive compilation of statistics relating to psychological type which has been taking place in America. Amongst those statistics are figures that raise our comments about psychological bias in the churches above the level of mere anecdote. Data collected by the Alban Institute indicates that, in terms of temperament, American Protestant clergy are highly unrepresentative of the population at large. What they found when they examined the four Keirsey–Bates temperament types was as follows:

Type	Clergy	US population
NF	41%	13%
SJ	35%	40%
NT	16%	12%
SP	8%	35%

Our own use of the Myers–Briggs Type Indicator, while on too small a scale to be statistically reliable, does seem to bear this out to some extent. In our experience the SP temperament is clearly under-represented in the church while the NF temperament is over-represented.

Local factors may also come into play. For example, explicitly traditionalist congregations do seem to be particularly attractive to the SJ temperament (the natural conservative). In their book *Personality Type and Religious Leadership*, Roy Oswald and Otto Kroeger suggest that some congregations may consist of up to 75 per cent SJs (as against 40 per cent in the population at large)! At times they even slip into language suggesting that the concept of temperament may be applied to entire congregations. But a church which caters primarily for a single temperament is no more to be admired than a church which caters exclusively for admirers of English choral music or, for that matter, heavy metal. The Church is not a place for meeting like-minded Christians or Christians who share our special interests. On the contrary, the Church should call us out of our personal ghettos to worship God in communion with people we would not, naturally speaking, mix with.

It does seem that the gospel is more attractive to some psychological types than others. Or, rather, *the ways in which we express* the gospel make it more accessible to some types than others. Clearly the lessons which we have learned in our missionary confrontation with other cultures need to be applied to this area of life as well.

We need to begin by reminding ourselves of the difference between evangelism and cultural imperialism. The psychological analogue of cultural imperialism is the approach which provides the new believer with a clear blueprint of a 'Christian personality'. Individual differences are brushed aside or suppressed in the relentless drive to make disciples. Such psychological imperialism is not the exclusive preserve of one particular branch of the Church. It may be found in certain fundamentalist groups but it was also a feature of the life of many traditional religious communities (at least prior to Vatican II).

Psychological imperialism often takes a less extreme form: the person whose temperament does not fit will be tolerated within the congregation. However, it will be clear to that person that they are merely tolerated. Their views are not taken seriously or elicit patronising responses. Churches may have their token mystics, intellectuals or evangelicals much as they may have token blacks or token women.

By contrast, genuine evangelism will take account of the other person's temperament. It will recognise it as an integral part of his or her God-given personality. It will seek to understand the ways in which that person's perception and judgement differ from our own and it will rejoice in the strengths which that person can offer to complement our weaknesses. But it will not forget that all human beings are fallen, that human sinfulness has implications for every aspect of what it means to be human including our temperament: that temperament is one of the factors that particularises sin so that this person tends to be self-righteous while that person tends to be self-indulgent, or self-deprecatory.

OUR COMMUNICATION PREFERENCES

Since the heart of Christianity is the good news it follows that communication is a matter of vital importance to us. Factors that affect the way in which we address others and which influence what those others perceive in our address must be taken into account in any consideration of evangelism.

Clearly many factors will affect the way we communicate: cultural factors, social factors. Equally clearly, we should not overlook the influence of psychological factors. And amongst the psychological factors are the ones picked out by Jung as the basis for his typology of personality.

Of the eight factors examined by the Myers–Briggs Indicator the four psychological functions will probably have the most direct effect on our communication with others. Sensing and intuition, our modes of perceiving, will play an important part in what we hear and see when we are addressed. Conversely, our preferred mode of perception is likely to influence our expectation of others' perceptions and hence colour the way in which we address others. Similarly our preferred mode of judgement will affect the way in which we pursue a line of argument or assess the arguments of others.

Sensing

As we have already pointed out several times, sensing simply refers to the straightforward use of the five senses. It is direct and simple. Such people are acutely observant of the facts of a situation.

This has clear implications for our communication preferences. If we are sensing types we will prefer to hear about facts and events. We will appreciate small details which root the account in everyday reality. Within the New Testament, Mark's Gospel is a good example of this approach: it is peppered with throwaway remarks, minor details which most commentators regard as superfluous. For example, only Mark tells us that the five thousand fed by Jesus sat down upon *green* grass (Mark 6:39): a minor detail but, for anyone who knows the Holy Land, it pinpoints rather precisely the time of year when this must have taken place. Mark is also the only evangelist to throw in the anecdote of the young man running away naked from the scene of Jesus' arrest.

What the sensing person wants is facts. They are unlikely to want to probe behind the facts. Thus allegorical spiritualising approaches to Scripture are unlikely to find a welcome with them. They may well be irritated by imaginative reconstructions of the gospel. Similarly the construction of an elaborate set of possibilities upon the foundation of an isolated verse of Scripture is likely to upset them.

Clearly the best evangelistic approach to a sensing type is likely to be direct and down-to-earth. It will stress the events of the gospel but will do so in a way that is fairly plain and unadorned. Above all it will avoid speculative flights of fancy!

Intuition

Where the sensing type focusses on the facts (for which the data from his senses are the prototype), the intuitive is much more interested in the facts behind the facts. For intuitives plain unadorned facts are simply boring: they are too obvious to be significant. Presented with a set of facts they will usually think (and perhaps ask outright), 'What are you getting at?

What's your angle?' What matters to them is not the facts themselves but the meaning they might bear.

Thus intuitives are incorrigible interpreters of facts. Within the philosophy of science there is a deep disagreement about the nature of scientific observations which corresponds rather closely to the division between sensing types and intuitives. There is a school of thought which regards observation as the process of acquiring straightforward facts about the world. In contrast to this is the view that there are no uninterpreted observations, that even the simplest act of measurement implies that certain decisions have been made about what is worth measuring (and hence a first step has already been taken in the process of interpretation). This latter view accords rather well with the intuitive approach to life.

Once again it has clear implications for preferences in communication. An intuitive will not appreciate a straightforward factual account of how it is. The story of St Augustine's pilgrimage to faith is a cautionary tale for all sensing types who would seek to witness to an intuitive. Augustine was a very gifted young man with a devout Christian mother (St Monica). Clearly she felt it her duty to teach her son the Christian faith. Augustine speaks of her suckling him on the name of Christ and yet he turned his back on Christianity partly out of contempt for what he regarded as the insultingly simple myths of the Bible. He had an insatiable desire for deeper meaning and he sought it in Hellenistic philosophy and esoteric religion. Still he was not satisfied. It was not until he came under the influence of the Bishop of Milan, St Ambrose, that he found what he was looking for: in Ambrose's teaching he found a Christianity transformed, a faith with more than enough depth to satisfy his longing for the facts behind the facts.

But being too factual (superficial as they would see it) is only one of the possible pitfalls when talking to intuitives. The other pitall is the temptation to explain too clearly the facts behind the facts. We said earlier that intuitives focus on the overall picture, the wood rather than the trees, but once they have been pointed in the right direction they can usually see the wood for themselves. There are few things that irritate them more than a sensing type labouring the point.

Jesus' use of parables in his teaching was a masterpiece of how to communicate with both sensing types and intuitives. His graphic portrayals of everyday situations might have been calculated to appeal to sensing types. But there was always the sting in the tail, the unexpected twist, the signal that there are facts behind the facts waiting to be perceived. And then there was the invitation to work it out for yourself: 'He who has ears to hear, let him hear' (Mark 4:9).

Thinking

This is the function which enables us to arrive at decisions via impersonal logic. A preference for thinking will be apparent in the way thinkers approach arguments. Apart from an overriding concern for truth, the main concern is likely to be that conclusions follow logically from the premises of the argument. Cause and effect will be important factors in their analyses of the world.

In presenting their case, thinkers are apt to be impersonal. They seek general arguments which can stand on their own apart from personal illustrations.

Combining thinking with sensing results in a temperament which revels in impersonal facts. Taken to extremes this can degenerate into the rationalism shown by some liberal theologians and also by some fundamentalists: that nit-picking concern for the finer points of Scripture which was once pilloried in the following terms:

These children can tell you who Huppim and Muppim and Ard were; they know the latitude of Beersheba, Kerioth and Beth-gamal; they can tell you who slew a lion in a pit on a snowy day; they have ripe views upon the identity of Nathanael and St Bartholomew; they can name the destructive miracles, the parables peculiar to St Luke, and, above all, they have a masterly knowledge of St Paul's second missionary journey. They are well loaded and ballasted with chronicles of Baasha and Zimri, Methuselah and Alexander the Coppersmith. . . . Therefore while our clergy are . . . instant in season and out of season . . . to proclaim the glories of Huppim and Muppim, the people are destroyed for lack of knowledge. . . . They know all about Abraham except the way to his bosom, all about David except his sure mercies, and all about St Paul except the faith which he preached and which justified him.[2]

Lest you think such things belong to a bygone era of Christian education, Lawrence once found himself forced to sit through a heated discussion on the identity of the forbidden fruit. Was it an apple, or an apricot, or a citron, or some other fruit?

Combining thinking with intuition produces an altogether more speculative type of thinker. Instead of focussing upon the precise meaning of a single Hebrew word this type will be more likely to amuse himself generating elaborate metaphysical systems. In the history of Christianity this outlook has given rise to a variety of gnostic heresies (belief systems in which salvation depends on the possession of secret knowledge about the nature of life, the universe, and everything).

The marvellously detailed angelologies of the Middle Ages were generated from remarkably little biblical material by just this sort of mind. Of course once such a system is established as fact it becomes the province of the ST as well, who will delight himself arguing about precisely how many angels can fit on the head of a pin!

Thinkers are likely to be attracted to the Christian faith by rational arguments. Theology textbooks are more likely to make them take Christianity seriously than any number of glowing personal testimonies. A staunchly evangelical friend who is now a missionary once surprised us by admitting that what originally attracted him to Christianity was a book by the liberal theologian Paul Tillich.

Feeling

The last of the four functions enables us to arrive at decisions by means of personal, aesthetic and ethical criteria. On its own this probably does not mean that the feeling type's presentation of an argument will be any less logical than their thinking counterpart. It must be remembered that feeling, as understood by Jung, is a rational function *complementing* thinking. Thus it has its own internal logic; its own standards of consistency and correspondence with reality. If this were not the case it would not be possible to discuss ethical matters rationally.

Where the thinker opts for an impersonal generalised presentation of eternal truths, the feeling type is likely to adopt a much more personal approach. This does not necessarily mean a disregard for truth. What it does mean is a commitment to the view that truth has to be encountered in a personal context.

The whole tenor of a feeling person's communication is likely to be warmer and more enthusiastic than that of the thinker. When preaching or witnessing they are more likely to stress their own personal experience since it is the point at which faith is most real for them. They are generally more sensitive to the needs and reactions of their hearers and, particularly if they are extraverts, will be prepared to adjust their presentation to meet the perceived needs.

Conversely a feeling person is more likely to appreciate such 'heart-warming' presentations of the gospel than a thinking person (who may be tempted to dismiss them as sentimental waffle). The charge of sentimentalism is one to watch. It is often levelled at feeling types who take their feeling preference to extremes.

Combined with sensing we get a temperament that is particularly interested in the specific details of personal experience. Such a combination may result in the sincere interest in individuals which can be such a boon in personal evangelism. This temperament may also lead a person into charitable activity inspired by individual cases of suffering. Taken to extremes it may degenerate into an exaggerated concern for personal religious experience.

If feeling is combined with intuition the result is a temperament with a greater interest in possibilities than in specifics. This is likely to result in a difference of emphasis when it comes to responding to the perceived needs of others. Where the SF responds directly to individual needs, the NF is more likely to perceive the facts behind the facts and address the structures that have given rise to those needs. Thus whereas the SF may be more inclined to traditional acts of charity, the NF may be more inclined to engage in social activism. There may well be a similar difference in their approach to matters spiritual. The SF tends to pietism but the NF may be drawn to some form of mysticism.

Any presentation of the gospel to feeling types must involve a personal dimension. It is not enough to expound the truth. They expect you to make clear how that truth affects you personally. In addition, they may be sensitive to the social implications of the gospel and will expect to see signs that you are responding to those implications.

The effect of the four attitudes

These generally have a less dramatic effect on the ways in which we communicate. Nevertheless they can still be important and useful pointers for how we might approach certain types of people can be gleaned from a consideration of them.

The *introvert* fears domination by the outside world. The claims of social institutions and individuals are perceived as threats to their personal integrity. Thus certain traditional forms of evangelism are likely to be counterproductive. Both mass rallies and the hard-sell approach adopted in some forms of personal witnessing could have been designed to heighten the introvert's fear of a loss of identity. Much more effective is a non-coercive setting: a *casual* conversation over coffee or a small group discussion (possibly Bible study or a discussion of some contemporary ethical issue with input from a Christian perspective). For the introvert the most important thing about the gospel is its capacity to set us free from the dead hand of society: the good news is that Jesus has liberated us from all that threatens to suppress who we are and that, through the Holy Spirit, we can achieve our God-given individuality.

If the introvert fears domination, the *extravert* fears alienation. Not surprisingly, alienation is the great bug-bear of our predominantly extravert western culture. The threat of isolation from self, from family or friends, from society as a whole is what disturbs this type. As you might expect the traditional forms of evangelism which may be ineffective with the introvert are likely to be just what the extravert needs. When you make that commitment to faith in Christ by walking forward at a Billy Graham rally you are very visibly joining a mass of other people who are taking the same step; you can see a whole new set of people to whom this action relates you. Similarly the positive side of the one-to-one hard sell is often a clearly expressed personal commitment to you and your spiritual well-being on the part of the evangelist. For the extravert, what matters about the gospel is not so much its power to liberate as its promise of new relationships and the fulfilment of old ones. The good news is that Jesus has called us into a new relationship with God and that, through that new relationship in the power of the Holy Spirit, all our other relationships are transformed (and that extends beyond our personal relationships to our relationship with society as a whole and our relationship with our environment and the entire material creation).

Finally *judging* and *perceiving* preferences will also have an impact on the way we communicate. Judging types like everything to be done decently and in order. A straightforward step-by-step unfolding of the gospel is more likely to appeal to them.

On the other hand, perceiving types are likely to find that boring. For them something which gives at least an impression of spontaneity is more attractive. A multi-media presentation with song and laser lights and audience participation may be what is required.

THE WHOLE GOSPEL FOR THE WHOLE PERSON

The point of this chapter is not that we must have sixteen different gospels for the sixteen different psychological types. On the contrary, there is one gospel but it is sufficiently rich to permit a presentation that engages *all* the psychological functions. We can see this by looking at some of the elements involved in proclaiming the gospel.

The telling of a story

First of all the gospel is a retelling of events. It is an account of things which actually happened in a particular time and at a particular place. Facts, historical events and details form an integral part of the good news. Without them Christianity would be no more than a myth to live by; attractive to intuitives, perhaps, but problematic for sensing types (particularly extraverts) who need to ground their faith in reality. The historical events of the gospel offer precisely that grounding in reality which sensing types seek.

The interpretation of events

But there is more to the gospel than bare unadorned historical facts. Every event recorded in the New Testament is packed with meaning beyond the simple fact of the event. There is a wealth of facts beyond facts to satisfy even the most demanding of intuitives. Thus, for example, we can readily agree with the Bishop of Durham's comment that there is more to the

94

resurrection than the resuscitation of a corpse. There certainly is! (On the other hand, if the truth of the resurrection is not built upon the revival of Jesus' corpse then we are back in the realms of mythology.)

It is the interpretation lying beyond the historical facts that enables the gospel to engage with intuitives as well as sensing types.

Extrapolation from the events

The next step is the logical extrapolation beyond the facts and their interpretation. This is the point at which the gospel engages with the thinking function.

Thus the fact of the empty tomb and its interpretation in the words, 'He has risen, he is not here; . . . he is going before you to Galilee' (Mark 16:6, 7), point beyond themselves. They force the listener to ask the question, 'What does it all mean?'

The personal impact of the events

The gospel is not just about something that took place in Palestine two millenia ago. When John the Baptist sent his message of doubt to Jesus the answer he received was in the form of a testimony: the deaf hear, the blind see, the lame walk. The gospel was objectively transforming lives then and it still does so today. Some account of the present power of the gospel is a legitimate part of today's proclamation. Such testimonies are the point at which the gospel engages with the feeling function.

Good news for extraverts and introverts

As we have already pointed out, the gospel is rich enough to address the characteristic fears of both introverts and extraverts. It offers the introvert freedom from the relationships that threaten to overwhelm his or her personal identity and it offers the extravert new relationships. This is not two separate messages but two aspects of the same message. We are set free from the ties that bind us to the path of rebellion against God (and, ultimately, are destructive of our personal identity) *and* introduced into a new set of relationships that unite us with our fellow Christians in the worship of God (and, ultimately, enable us to find who we truly are before God).

Good news for judgers and perceivers

The gospel is good news whether we approach the world with our judging function or our perceiving function. This is so because the reality of which it speaks is a living synthesis of order and spontaneity. The theologian Karl Barth once put it thus: 'God honours law as well as freedom. He loves the law-abiding bourgeois as well as the nomad.'[3]

The work of the Holy Spirit is decent and orderly but, at the same time, creative: the reality which God is creating is an ordered reality but that order is dynamic not static. It is always new.

Exercises

(a) Your testimony

Spend a few minutes reflecting on your own pilgrimage with God. Write down what you consider to be the significant landmarks in that journey. Perhaps you had a dramatic conversion experience or perhaps you came to a mature faith by a more gradual process. Describe that process, how your Christian faith has influenced your life, and what it means for you today.

Now reread your description in the light of all that we have said about psychological types. Alternatively, ask a friend who is familiar with the Myers–Briggs Type Indicator to read what you have written. In what ways does your description reflect your psychological type?

Is there anything in what you have written which might confuse or irritate someone of a different psychological type? Rewrite your description emphasising each of the psychological functions (sensing, intuition, thinking, and feeling) in turn.

(b) Your favourite hymns

Spend some time with a book of hymns and choruses selecting your favourites. Choose them on the basis of their words not their tunes.

What do you find attractive about them? Is there any correlation between your reasons for choosing these hymns (or choruses) and your psychological preferences? Do you think the writer shared those preferences? If not, does the overall tenor of the hymn give you any clues to the writer's preferences?

Does the book you have been using reflect a balance of the different preferences? Or does it appear to be weighted in favour of certain preferences rather than others?

Given the apparent preponderance of NFs amongst church-goers, one might expect popular hymn-books to be weighted in this direction. Why not scour your hymn-book for hymns and choruses which reflect other preferences, and see that they are used in worship from time to time?

6

Personality and Christian Leadership

As the title suggests we shall be concerned in this chapter with some of the implications of type theory for Christian leadership.

THE MYTH OF THE OMNICOMPETENT PASTOR

The monarchical view of pastoral care

Paradoxical as it may seem for a faith whose founder 'came not to be served but to serve' (Mark 10:45) and which initially exalted the concept of service, Christianity, at least in its western forms, has evolved an essentially monarchical understanding of the pastorate. Perhaps this was inevitable in view of the close relationship between the Church and political power throughout western Europe from the time of the Roman Emperor Constantine until relatively recently. Indeed the last vestiges of this connection are still to be seen in the form of establishment enjoyed by the Church of England to this day.

But even before the Constantinian establishment of Christianity as the state religion of Rome significant moves had been made in this direction. The understanding of priesthood and ministry which was already developing within the western Church was a hierarchical one. Again this is, perhaps, understandable. The early Church was frequently persecuted and found it very easy to think of itself as a beleaguered army battling against a hostile world. In such circumstances it was natural enough for them to model themselves upon human armies. In the generation immediately following the Apostles, Clement of Rome could exhort his readers to 'enthusiastically accept military service' in the army of Christ and point out that 'each man in his rank carries out the orders of the emperor or the leaders'. His younger contemporary, Ignatius of Antioch, offered an even more striking image of hierarchy: 'be eager to act always in godly concord; with the bishop presiding as the counterpart of God, the presbyters as the counterpart of the council of the apostles, and the deacons (most dear to me) who have been entrusted with a service under Jesus Christ.' A later Church leader, St Cyprian, could simply assert that all heresy stemmed from 'the failure to have one in the church who is looked upon as the temporal representative of Christ as priest and judge.'

Thus in the episcopal traditions (Orthodoxy, Roman Catholicism, Lutheranism, Anglicanism, and Methodism) the minister has traditionally been understood as one set over the congregation. In Presbyterianism a similar distinction was preserved with the minister being set over against the congregation. Only in congregational forms of church government has this monarchical view been supplanted.

It is hardly surprising to find that this view has made a deep impression on English thought. Even when the notion of the pastor as a monarch (the sole leader) is radicalised by reference back to New Testament teaching on the leader as servant, there remains the feeling that one person should bear sole responsibility for the life of the church. For George Herbert it meant that the minister should make himself indispensable: 'The Country Parson desires to be all to his parish, and not only a pastor, but a lawyer also, and a physician.' And we might add to that list schoolmaster and magistrate.

Such an outlook is by no means a thing of the past. Everywhere ministers are struggling to live up to their own and their congregations' expectations of omnicompetence. Only a decade ago David Watson commented that, the vicar, or minister, is usually the bottleneck, if not the cork of his church: nothing can go in or out except through him. No meetings can take place unless he is the leader or chairman. No decisions can be made without his counsel and approval. I know of some parishes where the laity cannot meet even for Bible study or prayer unless the vicar is present.[1]

Unrealistic expectations?

What do we expect of our ministers?

First and foremost we expect our ministers to proclaim the word of the Lord. We imagine (or, at least, hope) that the art of preaching will have been an important component of their training. Within this area, the Church of England's ordinal makes specific reference to calling their hearers to repentance: evangelism is an explicit part of the ordained ministry.

More generally the minister is expected to teach the Christian faith by word and example. The skills required for this task will vary considerably depending on the size and nature of the group. Large groups demand a mastery of voice production (and possibly of the art of sermon construction). More intimate groups call for sensitivity and flexibility to meet the needs of the individuals present. But whatever the size of the group we will probably expect our minister to be studious in his preparations.

Another set of skills is demanded by our expectation that the minister be responsible for leading public worship. More often than not, in addition to acting as the worship leader, the minister will have chosen the hymns (and possibly the readings), preached the sermon, led the intercessions: in fact, organised and run every aspect of the service. He or she may even have typed and duplicated the service sheets. We know of one or two cases where, in addition to all this, the minister also doubles as the organist!

Apart from being skilled in the leading of public worship we rightly expect our ministers to be men and women of prayer. In the Anglican ordinal they are explicitly called to intercede for their congregations.

Finally there is the entire area of pastoral care. We expect our ministers to be able and willing to offer spiritual counsel to all who need it. We expect them to minister in appropriate ways to 'the poor, the needy, the sick, and all who are in trouble'. To this category of expectations we might add the pastoral offices such as baptisms, weddings, and funerals.

Institutional expectations

It is an inescapable fact that our churches are both expressions of the Church (i.e., a community called into existence by God) and human institutions. In addition to the spiritual tasks expected of our ministers there are usually a number of temporal institutional expectations. This is particularly noticeable in those churches which pay their clergy. Here the clergyperson is also the paid official of the congregation, presbytery, diocese or denomination. Often he or she is the only full-time paid Christian worker in that congregation.

Under such circumstances it is very easy for the minister to be seen as the chief executive and administrator of the congregation. As such he or she is ultimately responsible for servicing the institutional structures of the church. Thus the minister is expected to chair (or at least attend) all the committees (or at least the ones that make significant decisions). The ministers may end up being responsible for the fabric of the church buildings. They are the ones to whom the central heating engineers, electricians, glaziers, death-watch beetle exterminators, etc., report.

The ministers very often also have a monopoly over church communications. They are the ones who are responsible for making announcements during public worship. More often than not they also have a significant say in the content of the church magazine or newsletter. In fact they may well find that they have to edit and print the newsletter.

Finally, as the chief executive of the congregation, the minister is also its ultimate policy maker. This is at the heart of David Watson's complaint about ministerial bottlenecks. Since the minister is responsible for teaching and worship there can be no developments or innovations here without his or her active approval. But this control may extend beyond these areas. The minister often chairs the church's decision-making body. In fact, we know of one clergyman who is also secretary and treasurer of his parochial church council!

The impossibility of omnicompetence

It must be clear from the preceding that it is simply unrealistic to expect one man or woman (or even a small professional team) to tackle all that is expected of a typical Christian minister. There are simply too many tasks requiring too many differing skills.

Unfortunately many of our models of ministry are drawn from earlier eras, e.g., George Herbert's *The Country Parson* and Richard Baxter's *The Reformed Pastor* are still in print. It may have been possible for ministers to encompass all the tasks laid out above (with varying degrees of success) in a slower, less pressurised age. Before the nineteenth century most British ministers probably had only a few hundred parishioners under their care. And even the busiest of eighteenth-century itinerant preachers, John Wesley, estimated that he had up to ten hours a day to himself (largely because of the slowness of horse and carriage).

Such small parishes and such a slow pace of life are a thing of the past. In some suburban parishes it would not be unusual for the vicar to be responsible for several baptisms and funerals a week (not to mention three or four weddings every Saturday afternoon throughout the summer) quite apart from the regular

Sunday services, teaching programme, and routine pastoral care. This is simply a function of the size of the parish.

Similarly the ease of communications has dramatically altered the lifestyle of most vicarages. The vicar is now available to any parishioner at virtually any time of the day or night. All they have to do is pick up the telephone and push a few buttons.

Even if it were desirable for a small élite of professional Christian ministers to exercise an omnicompetent ministry, the pressures of modern life have rendered it impossible. In the average church, there are simply too many things needing to be done too soon for the myth of omnicompetence to be maintained with any degree of realism.

PREACHING AND TEACHING . . . AND TYPE

As we have already seen, personality can affect how we communicate and, hence, how we hear and proclaim the gospel. Clearly it will also be relevant to how we preach and teach.

Preaching to different personalities

Someone once suggested that, in order to cater for all personality types, a sermon must contain elements which engage with all four of the psychological functions. Thus the 'ideal sermon' will be rooted in concrete realities to engage with the sensing function. It will contain unspoken possibilities waiting to be perceived by our intuition. It will be intellectually stimulating for the benefit of thinkers. And it will be heart-warming, engaging with our feeling function.

Clearly this is a counsel of perfection. Very few of us are capable of giving equal weight to all four functions. On the other hand, most of us could improve our sermons by paying more attention to those functions with which we are less comfortable.

Thus sensing preachers could discipline themselves to leave

some things unsaid. They would do well to remember that adults do not need to be spoon-fed. Conversely intuitive preachers could take greater pains to earth their sermons with concrete illustrations. When Lawrence was an undergraduate he attended a church with an outstanding preacher. However, it was often said of that preacher that many members of the adult congregation got more out of his children's talks than out of the sermon proper. He was probably an intuitive since he tended to leave too much unsaid when addressing an adult congregation.

Similarly thinkers should always ask themselves whether their sermons read more like lectures. One way of redressing the balance would be to study biographies and autobiographies: illustrations drawn from life experiences are an invaluable source of the human interest which is so important to feeling types. And again, preachers whose sermons are full of human interest and heart-warming inspirational stories would do well to ask from time to time, 'What truth am I trying to convey?'

In fact we would all do well to ask ourselves, 'What is the point of a sermon?' It is only too easy to let our psychology rather than our theology determine the purpose of sermons. To be specific, we may allow our preferred judging function to determine what we regard as the purpose of a sermon. This comes across most clearly in the case of thinkers: for them a sermon is primarily for the communication of some truth; it is an opportunity for teaching. Thus in some churches the sermon can become a lecture. In fact, we have heard of one parish in which the official title of the curate is 'Lecturer' precisely because he has traditionally been responsible for a significant proportion of the preaching. On the other hand feeling types may consider that the real purpose of the sermon is to bring about some change in the hearts of their congregation. At its most degenerate this may give rise to the sermon as entertainment. However, we believe it may also be the motivation behind the evangelistic sermon: the sermon designed to provoke a moment of crisis and a decision for or against faith in

Christ. In a similar way the manipulative sermon is born: the sermon which seeks to alter the everyday actions and behaviour of members of the congregation.

While not wishing to criticise teaching, evangelism, behaviour modification or entertainment in the right contexts, we do have doubts about whether any of these should be the primary purpose of a sermon preached as an integral part of an act of worship. Surely it is the act of worship itself which should be ultimate. The function of the sermon is to draw people further into the worship of God. This can be by way of their thinking function as the sermon offers them fresh insight into the being and character of God. Alternatively it can be by way of their feeling function as the preacher leads them into a deeper experience of God's grace and love.

Teaching and type

The distinction between preaching and teaching is an important one. While the latter can be quite impersonal (e.g., lectures to large audiences) it is fundamentally a more personal form of instruction. Jesus' Sermon on the Mount was preaching; what he did with the Twelve as he shared his life with them was teaching. Similarly the great philosophical schools of ancient Greece relied heavily upon a personal dialogue between teacher and pupil.

Clearly this sort of teaching is more likely to be found in the small groups of a church rather than in its pulpit. Small groups can more effectively tackle the issues that really matter to the group members at the level appropriate to the group. We are not restricted by the context (e.g., dialogue between preacher and congregation is virtually impossible from a pulpit) and can adopt whatever method is most appropriate. Because it is smaller and more personal, the small group (housegroup, home group, cell group, Bible study, catechumenate, or whatever you like to call it) also offers the personal support which can be vital if insight is to bear fruit in changed lives.

The effect of temperament on learning

Temperament[2] has a noticeable influence on the way in which different people like to learn. This could be usefully borne in mind when organising housegroups. What is the ideal setting for one person may seem boring or threatening to others.

Epimethean (SJ). This is the commonest of the temperaments. Such people tend to be orderly, accurate, industrious, reliable, thorough, trustworthy. Their chief characteristic is loyalty to the established way of doing things.

SJs are likely to be the backbone of the local church both numerically and in terms of commitment (just as they are the backbone of every other human institution). They are also likely to be the ones who resist any change in the way things are done. They need to be convinced that the changes will increase the orderliness and efficiency of the institution without radically altering its character.

When it comes to learning, they prefer teachers who have some degree of authority. They are likely to feel more comfortable if housegroup leaders are officially recognised in some way and possess some genuine authority within the congregation. At the same time such leaders must be worthy of respect in the sense that they somehow embody the values of the institution and display a certain competence in what they do. Thus housegroup leaders might be closely associated with the lay leadership of the congregation (e.g., the diaconate or eldership). They might also be expected to be mature Christians who are involved in Christian education themselves (perhaps through a housegroup leaders' housegroup).

In the absence of such authoritative leaders an alternative might be some form of workbook. In any case what SJs understand by teaching is the passing on of clearly defined information by an authoritative other.

Dionysian (SP). Although common in the wider community, people of this temperament are relatively scarce within the church. Such people live for pleasure and may well dismiss the Church as too rule bound and formal to satisfy their needs.

SPs positively dislike lectures, predetermined structures and learning packages. They learn best in situations which give them hands-on experience. Thus they tend to do better at practical subjects than abstract ones.

For example, imagine an evangelism training course. The SJ would expect it to consist of a systematic progression through all the situations you are likely to meet together with advice on how to tackle them. By contrast, the SP would learn much more effectively by being given a pile of tracts and sent out into the streets alongside an experienced evangelist. SPs learn on the job.

They also enjoy performance. If you can work drama, music, collage, or other practical creative activities into your teaching programme you are much more likely to engage the attention of this type.

Apollonian (NF). This type seems to be much commoner in the Church than in the population at large. They are also very common in the teaching profession (where they tend towards the more radical student-oriented methods).

For NFs a housegroup (like any other learning situation) should also be a support group. After all, learning is ultimately about discovering and developing their own identity. The things they care about include commitment to one another, social development, and caring. They are likely to be in the forefront of any initiative to increase the local church's service to the community at large.

Thus they may expect greater social responsibility than SPs. On the other hand they are likely to want a more democratic approach than that of the SJ. Not for them the authoritative figure who produces the right answer. For them housegroup leaders should be equals, fellow pilgrims in the journey of discovery which is Christianity.

They are great believers in the value of everyone's contribution. Every member of a housegroup has unique insights and experiences which can enrich the group as a whole. Thus the method of 'instruction' within the housegroup should not be the more traditional didactic one preferred by SJs but one of more open discussion.

Promethean (NT). This type may initially show a preference for either of the learning situations preferred by SJs and NFs. The traditional didactic approach appeals to the NT's liking for clear logical structures. However, the NT needs the freedom to disagree with the conclusions of the argument. Information will not be accepted merely because it is conveyed by someone in authority. A more open discussion-based approach appeals to the NT's interest in different possibilities and perspectives. However, they soon become irritated if the discussion fails to achieve any visible intellectual progress, if it merely 'goes round in circles'.

Since they are the archetypal intellectuals they are most at home with the methods which have been developed in academic environments since time immemorial: lectures, seminars, problem-centred discussions and dialogue. A more modern method which we might add to this list is brainstorming.

TYPE AND PASTORAL COUNSELLING

One of the temptations when using the Myers–Briggs Type Indicator (or similar psychometric devices) is to attempt to spot a 'best' type for a particular role. This may be done either by examining statistical evidence (how many people of this type opt into that role?) or on a theoretical basis (given our definition of this or that type in what areas might we expect them to excel?). As a result, some businesses misuse the Indicator in order to select particular types for particular jobs.

However, it should be recalled that type is a matter of preference not skill. This is very clear in the case of the thinking function. Although we tend to associate thinking with intelligence and academic ability, there appears to be little correlation between academic achievement and a preference for thinking. Up to half of the population might be expected to have a preference for thinking. This does not indicate the existence of millions of frustrated Einsteins!

Since type indicates preference it is reasonable to assume that those occupations which attract large numbers of a specific type are in some way congenial to people of that type. Many people appreciate a logical analytical approach to decision making but only a tiny proportion of them will have the skills which make an Einstein.

It is important to remember this in connection with things that are sometimes said about type and aptitude for pastoral counselling. Statistically it is clear that certain psychological types are especially attracted to counselling. In particular, extraverts who perceive by intuition and prefer to make judgements by feeling find it a congenial occupation. Other types (particularly introverts) may feel less comfortable when faced with this task. However, this does not mean that they are necessarily less competent. What it may mean is that they find such situations more stressful. We need to recognise the value of the other skills that such 'non-standard' types could bring to the task. For, in the case of pastoral counselling, we should not underestimate the sheer variety of situations which may arise.

Extraversion and introversion

We might expect people attracted to pastoral care and counselling to be extraverts. They are naturally sociable and find it relatively easy to start and maintain conversations. Thus many people find them easier to approach than introverts.

The danger with extravert counsellors is that they may be too sociable, too talkative. Introverts, in particular, may find extraverts rather overpowering. There are times when the situation demands a gentler approach. Of course, if the extravert is also a feeling person they may be sufficiently sensitive to the other person's needs to give them that room.

Introverts may be less comfortable about finding themselves called upon to advise or counsel. On the other hand, they are more likely to give the other person a chance to speak. This is because they themselves need silence in which to put ideas into words.

Sensing and intuition

Intuition is the more penetrating of the two modes of perception. It sees beyond the superficial details to the underlying patterns. Thus you might expect intuitive counsellors to be much better at getting to the heart of the matter.

The problem with intuition is that it will seek patterns even when there are none. In some cases it may look beyond the real problems and perceive quite illusory problems. Earlier we described intuitives as seeing the facts beyond the facts! At times they may instead see the fantasy beyond the facts! An instructive fictional example of this danger is the character of Jonathan Darrow in Susan Howatch's novel *Glamorous Powers*. She portrays the breakdown of a highly intuitive personality during which Darrow, who has the gift of spiritual healing, becomes involved in both real and imaginary exorcisms.

The monk who acts as a foil to Darrow in that novel (and who, in the end, rescues him from his own folly) is also instructive. Susan Howatch has cast a sensing person in that role. He is consistently sceptical of Darrow's intuitions, visions, and acts of healing. In the end it is his welcome breath of realism that brings healing to the destructive situation created by Darrow's intuition.

It is precisely that breath of realism which is the sensing person's particular contribution to pastoral care. Instead of tackling possibly imaginary spiritual difficulties they will address themselves to the visible problems which have caused the person to seek counselling.

As ever the complementary nature of the two functions is clear. Sensing alone may lead to a superficial form of counselling in which the symptoms are tackled while the underlying problem is left untouched. On the other hand, intuition alone may lead into a dangerous fantasy world of imagined psychological and spiritual problems.

Thinking and feeling

In many situations we might expect feeling to be the more appropriate form of judgement. We expect feeling people to be more sensitive, more caring. They find it relatively easy to establish a rapport with the other person. Such people are sometimes said to have 'the heart of a pastor'.

Thinking types, on the other hand, are generally seen as cold and analytical. People may find them unsympathetic or even confrontational. However, there are pastoral situations in which these are precisely the characteristics needed by the pastor!

For example, sin is not something to be understood and treated as an unfortunate ailment. If the pastor is convinced that a person's sinful behaviour is at the heart of a particular problem then the appropriate way forward is confrontation. That person must be made to face the sinfulness of their behaviour and given the opportunity to repent and experience God's grace.

Other pastoral situations demand the ability to analyse complex problems in a logical fashion. Consider, for example, someone who is caught in a tangled maze of debt. Tea and sympathy is not enough. He or she needs someone to cut through the confusion and give them practical advice on what to do about their problem.

Judging and perceiving

Once again both attitudes can be of value in different pastoral situations.

A preference for judging, with its associated desire to bring order out of chaos, can be helpful in many pastoral situations. Remember that judging does not mean judgemental, it means a desire for order and control over the environment. Where this could come into its own might be in umpiring group counselling sessions. For example, in family or marriage counselling it is helpful to have a counsellor who can help the people being counselled to avoid the ever-decreasing circles of mutual recrimination. Judging types are more inclined to move the conversation along and to prevent clients from going fruitlessly over and over the same ground.

On the other hand the judging person's penchant for order can be inappropriate at times. The curate who allots precisely ten minutes to each bed when hospital visiting may get through his visiting list efficiently, but what impression does it leave with the people he is supposed to be caring for? Similarly the vicar who adopts an appointments system must beware of importing into his pastoral care the impersonality of a dentist's waiting room.

Many pastoral problems call for the flexibility of a perceiving type. Such people come into their own when forced to make a rapid response to some crisis. They are also likely to seem less threatening than their more efficient judging counterparts. Like introverts they may well make good listeners, though for very different reasons (perceiving people like to know what the case is and feel little responsibility for making decisions about it). They may prefer the less directive forms of counselling. And, of course, their pastoral weaknesses are precisely the converse of those facing the judging type: they must discipline themselves to be directive when the situation calls for it.

Conclusion

The point of the preceding sections has been to stress that nobody is excluded from engaging in pastoral care by virtue of their psychological type. Type is only a matter of preference. All of us are capable of using the functions we find less congenial. Thus, although certain types of people are naturally attracted to pastoral care, it is equally important for would-be pastors to have the ability to operate out of type with ease that comes with personal maturity.

TYPE AND ADMINISTRATION

We recently heard someone comment that, 'Our Lord called the Twelve to be fishers of men while our seminaries are content with producing aquarium keepers.' That person certainly had a point. Once you get into the average parish, there does seem to be far more emphasis on maintaining the structures of the local church than on increasing the borders of Christ's Kingdom. On the other hand the comment is unfairly dismissive of the administration which is necessary to keep any human institution running smoothly.

It is also rather misleading about our theological colleges. One recent report on theological training actually criticised colleges for failing to give students a sufficiently concrete understanding of what the Church is. Many Christian leaders appear to have a rather abstract mystical concept of the Church which is hard to relate to the local church. Perhaps if we recalled that ours is an incarnational faith, we would achieve a more satisfactory connection between the one holy catholic and apostolic Church of the creeds and St Philip's down the road. The point is that the Church of the creeds has to be incarnated in the local church. It is as we express holiness, catholicity and apostolicity in our local churches that the Church becomes real. And, since local churches are human institutions, administration (the art of aquarium keeping) is an integral part of that reality.

The routine paperwork

The church's budget and the maintenance of the fabric both generate a good deal of routine paperwork. So do such things as maintaining a membership list. In the case of the Church of England there is also the paperwork associated with baptisms, marriages, and funerals.

It is very easy, in our more spiritual moments, to dismiss all this paperwork as missing the point of what the church is about. Nevertheless it is an essential part of maintaining the structures which give concrete reality to our more spiritual notions of the Church. Clearly there is something wrong if it eats up an inordinate amount of our time and energy. Conversely, we are equally wrong to neglect paperwork in the belief that it doesn't matter. Sooner or later it will matter, when the tax inspectors start asking questions about your covenant scheme or when a failure to obtain the necessary licence upsets someone's wedding plans.

Ideally all this routine paperwork should be handled efficiently and unobtrusively. It calls for someone who enjoys dealing with facts; someone who takes an analytical and decisive approach to life. As you might expect statistical studies based on the Myers–Briggs Type Indicator show that certain types do have a marked preference for work of this sort. Perhaps the most striking study was a survey of school administrators: 86 per cent proved to be judging types. Other studies indicate that people whose type is ESTJ or ISTJ find routine administration particularly congenial.

However, we should not forget the cautionary note of the previous section. People of this type may enjoy routine administration more than other types. But this does not mean that people who dislike paperwork are less competent at it. Lawrence (INTJ) and Diana (ESFJ) both dislike routine pàperwork

114

but see it as a necessary evil to be dealt with as quickly and accurately as possible so that they are then free to do the things that do matter to them.

Policy making

Administration is more than routine paperwork. This is because the church as a human institution is more than a static bureaucracy. It has to grow and adjust to the needs of a rapidly changing society. It has to re-present the gospel in ways that are intelligible and relevant to this society. Thus merely being able to file the facts away in the right places is not sufficient.

'Where there is no vision, the people perish' (Prov. 29:18, KJV). This may not be the most accurate translation of this particular verse but it does offer a very apt commentary on the poverty of any bureaucracy. Human institutions need a sense of direction, they need visions of the future towards which they are moving.

This is the realm of policy making. In most secular institutions it is regarded as a form of administration. We believe that the Church has rightly regarded this as an important aspect of spiritual leadership: in spiritual terms, it is the prophetic ministry.

What has personality to do with prophecy? Surely it is a gift of the Holy Spirit bestowed as God sees fit. This is certainly true. Nevertheless God does not completely disregard the natural gifts he has bestowed on his people when distributing supernatural ones. As we pointed out earlier, intuition does seem to be associated with what we might call a natural capacity for prophecy. Intuitives who have spotted trends in politics, economics or science long before their contemporaries are often regarded as secular prophets. If he chooses, God can take such a natural gift and use it to guide his people.

Perhaps that is why there is such a stress on discernment of prophecy in the New Testament. There may well be occasions on which apparently prophetic statements are no more than

115

the product of a natural psychological function. Indeed the same individual may sometimes utter genuinely prophetic statements under God's guidance while at other times making similar statements which are no more than his or her natural insight.

A caring institution

Another point to bear in mind when talking about administration in connection with the church is that the church is not a business or a government department. Efficiency is a virtue but it should not be given the absolute status it is sometimes accorded in secular circles.

Within the Church, efficiency must play a subservient role to the Church's mission. That is the truth behind the aquarium keeping jibe. The structures should not be so obtrusive that they obscure the proclamation, service, and worship which lie at the heart of the Church's mission.

The efficiency of the sensate thinking (ST) types who enjoy the routine paperwork has to be balanced by the vision of intuitives and the sensitivity of feeling types. We need feeling types to remind us that efficient administration is only a relative value. They are aware of and remind others of the needs of individuals, of the congregation, and of the wider society.

WHY WE NEED EACH OTHER

Complementarity of opposites

Again and again we have noticed in preceding sections how one function or attitude or type gives rise to tendencies which are balanced by its opposite. This has given rise to the widespread use of the Myers–Briggs Type Indicator in the development of teamwork. Although every individual possesses the capacity to use all of the functions it is rare to find people who can apparently use all of them with ease. Thus in any complex venture which requires the exercise of a variety of functions a smoothly working team can be a great help.

Extraverts and introverts can work together for mutual benefit. This is particularly clear in marriage. An introvert who is married to an extravert may well find that the contacts created by the extravert enable them to make far more friends than was previously the case. The extravert brings increased breadth to the life of the introvert. Conversely the introvert brings new depth to the life of an extravert.

Sensing types and intuitives complement each other's perceptions of the world or the project they have been asked to tackle. The sensing type has a much keener awareness of what is in fact the case. An S can detail the symptoms of the problem accurately, he or she knows precisely what the fine print in the contract says. The sensing type can also help the intuitive to appreciate and enjoy the present reality. When it comes to problem-solving sensing types are particularly good at applying past experience.

Where sensing types remind us of the riches of the past, intuitives alert us to the possibilities of the future. We need them to penetrate to the very roots of the problem, and to provide the vision which gives direction and meaning to our work.

Thinkers and feelers need each other: the analytical powers of the one complement the sensitivity of the other.

Apart from logical analysis the thinker will bring to any project a penchant for spotting the errors before they are committed, a degree of consistency, and the firmness to make sure that unpleasant decisions are actually carried out.

Feeling types will ensure that the interests and needs of real people are not overlooked by the project. They bring humanity to our decision making. Because of their sensitivity to an audience they are often much better communicators than thinking types. Thus they are invaluable in persuading, bringing reconciliation, and arousing enthusiasm.

Judging and perceiving types also complement each other.

117

An emphasis on judging will ensure that we get things done. Judging types will encourage us to plan properly and make decisions at the appropriate times. On the other hand, perceiving types will bring a valuable element of flexibility to any team. They will point out any new factors that need to be considered and will help us to avoid premature decisions.

The priesthood of all believers

The notion that people of different temperament are complementary is not specifically Christian. In fact, it probably owes as much to Jung's penchant for mysticism as it does to any parental influence (his father was a clergyman).

However, similar sentiments can be found in the pages of the New Testament as witness the title of Chapter 1. We are all incorporated into a single body: all our apparently contradictory strengths and gifts and weaknesses are meant to work in harmony within the body of Christ.

A similar concept is that of the New Testament understanding of priesthood. The New Testament envisages all Christians as priests. We are *all* called (without distinctions of class, or race, or sex) to some specific priestly ministry. The resulting variety of ministries is held in unity by the fact that they are all initiated and empowered by the one Holy Spirit.

Although most churches pay lip-service to the concept of a priesthood of all believers few, in the past, have taken it seriously. The exceptions have tended to be radical Protestant groups such as the Quakers or the Brethren. However, there has been a revival of interest in the concept in recent years. In part this has been due to the charismatic renewal: lay people have discovered that the Holy Spirit enables them to perform tasks which previously they had regarded as the exclusive preserve of the ordained minister. Another factor has been the pressure to ordain women. Beyond any merely fashionable feminism, this movement has raised fundamental questions about the nature of Christian ministry. Perhaps one of the most telling slogans of the movement is, 'The problem is not the ordination of women, but the ordination of men.' That problem will not be brushed aside merely by opening an exclusive male club to selected women.

The priesthood of all believers does not invalidate an ordained priesthood but it does relativise it. It reminds us that the ordained priesthood is representative, that, in order to maintain decency and good order, it seems right to call out from our midst and train certain individuals to function as our representatives, the focal points of our worship.

It also transforms our understanding of baptism and confirmation. They are the rites of initiation. But initiation into what? If we take the priesthood of all believers seriously, they are the services by which we are ordained as Christian priests. Thus, whatever else they might imply, they should certainly lead us to look seriously for the ministry to which God is calling us.

Exercise

Your ideal pastor

Spend a few minutes thinking about what you expect in a pastor/minister/parish priest. List as many qualities and functions as you can.

Now reconsider your list in the light of type theory. Try to determine which psychological preferences would most naturally give rise to these qualities or enable a minister to perform these functions.

In the light of this exercise do you regard your list as realistic?

7

Transcending Temperament

A Jungian View of Personal Growth

Fundamental to Jung's work on the human psyche (or soul)
was a particular understanding of the process of psychological
growth and development. Every human being, he believed,
undergoes a more or less clearly defined process of development towards psychological maturity. The name given to this
process by Jung and his followers is *individuation*.

Within a typical human lifespan Jung discerned four clear
phases. The periods of *childhood* and *youth* are periods in
which the individual comes to terms with their individual and
social environment. At first, during childhood, the new centre
of personality is entirely immersed within the attitudes and
values of the family. It remains within the psychological womb
of the family. Jung himself described the child as 'not yet
completely born, but . . . still enclosed in the psychic atmosphere of its parents.'[1] Psychological birth or the transition to
youth is related to the onset of sexual awareness at puberty.
The physiological changes which overtake us entail corresponding psychological changes: notably we become (sometimes
painfully) aware of others. During the period of youth our self-
definition over against parental influences and our quest for a
place within the larger community become pressing problems.
Taken together childhood and puberty represent our journey
outwards into the world.

There is not always a clear point of transition from youth to
the next major period, *maturity*. During this period we make

120

our own way in the world. We find out who we are. We carve out a niche for ourselves within the community and the world of work. Perhaps we meet a life partner; Jung certainly regarded the propagation of the race and the care of children as part of the work of this period.

However, maturity brings with it other goals besides these purely natural ones. We come to realise that there is more to life than money making, social achievement, and child-bearing. Jung suggested that this 'more' could be sought in human culture. His belief that there was 'more' to life and that its discovery was a vital part of the second half of life laid the foundation for that thoroughly modern concept, the mid-life crisis. In his own words, 'we cannot live the afternoon of life according to the programme of life's morning; for what was great in the morning will be little at evening, and what in the morning was true will at evening have become a lie.'[2]

As we progress through maturity to old age so the focus of our life shifts from the external world of material success to matters pertaining to eternity. Jung himself suggested that the shift was from nature to culture or from life to death: we begin to prepare ourselves for death and what may or may not transpire thereafter. It is no coincidence that in most cultures the elders are the bearers of the religious mysteries of the culture. Childhood and youth are times for the material; maturity and old age are times for the spiritual. The journey outwards must give way to a journey inwards as we explore the aspects of our soul neglected in youth.

Individuation and temperament

Virtually every aspect of Jung's work can be related back to this central theme of psychological development or individuation. For example, he is well known for his interest in the symbolism of dreams: that interest derived from his belief that dreaming was an important mechanism for the encouragement of individuation. Not surprisingly we find that both Jung and his

121

followers also had clear views about the role of temperament or personality type in personal growth.

In the context of the Myers–Briggs Type Indicator it is usually assumed that the preferred functions (your dominant and auxiliary) will develop first. Preferences may appear quite clearly in childhood (e.g., our eldest child, at six, shows every sign of becoming an intuitive type). However, such preferences may be erratic at this stage. The priority for the period of youth is seen as establishing a clear type preference and developing one's skill in the use of the preferred functions. With a firm foundation it is then possible to turn, in maturity and old age, to an exploration of the functions which have earlier been neglected. Thus the thinker might begin to explore his or her feelings and values; or the sensing type may find ways of developing intuition, perhaps through some form of artistic expression (e.g., Lawrence's father, a retired civil engineer who is unmistakably ESTJ, has in recent years devoted a good deal of time to developing his skills as a painter of water-colours).

Some Jungians have tried to define this process even more closely. One such model suggests that the dominant function is developed during childhood, the auxiliary during adolescence, and so on. Furthermore this model suggests that we also tend to switch between extraversion and introversion as we move from one phase to the next.

Individuation and spiritual maturity

The main way in which Jung's views on personal growth relate to Christian spirituality is in reminding us that people do grow! What may be appropriate for one person may be quite wrong for another. This may help to explain why Christians sometimes find that the patterns of prayer and Bible study which have nourished them for years no longer seem to satisfy them. Such crises in people's prayer lives are not necessarily triggered by unacknowledged sin as some Christians seem to think. It may simply be that their prayer crisis reflects a psychological crisis. Sadly the Christian churches do not have a good track record when it comes to handling such crises. Most of us will know Christians who have found it impossible to carry on in the same tradition. Indeed some readers may have converted from evangelicalism to Roman Catholicism or vice versa.

Jung's presentation of the latter half of life as a journey inwards, an exploration of the spiritual dimension of life, is one that resonates with many contemporary concerns. There is much talk of self-realisation, of achieving our full human potential. This is one of the driving forces behind the contemporary resurgence of interest in spirituality. Indeed, from the descriptions offered by some commentators, one might almost think that society as a whole were embarking on a journey inwards: a social analogue of Jung's ideas of individual development.

Nevertheless, in spite of its usefulness as a tool for understanding some spiritual crises and the contemporary popularity of such ideas, Christians must approach Jung's model of personal growth with caution.

For Jung, psychological development is a natural process. What is happening as an individual matures is nothing other than the unfolding of innate potential. There is nothing laudable about the process: it is just as inevitable as the physiological changes which occur at puberty. And, as with physiological growth, any failures are treated as pathological: the person is sick not evil.

Confusion arises because psychology has pushed the notion of development into the realms of morality and spirituality. The work of Kohlberg and, more recently, James Fowler suggests that just as we grow physically and mentally so we grow ethically and spiritually. Christian theology has made similar claims for centuries. However, there is a danger in their tendency to make grace superfluous. Ethical and spiritual growth become entirely natural processes under our own control (at least in the negative sense that we can hinder our growth). It is but a short step from this position to the view of many in the human potential movement that salvation is achieved by our own efforts.

A Christian View of Personal Growth

There is a Christian alternative to the secular models of personal growth to which Jung contributed so much. However, it is not often recognised as an alternative today. The reason for this lack of recognition lies in the fact that to see it we must shift the focus of our attention quite radically.

The Christian gospel calls attention away from the individual personality. Self-fulfilment is no longer the main item on the agenda. Self is no longer the centre of our concerns. In place of self, the gospel offers a new centre of attention, namely, God. But it is very specific about the God who can be a satisfying substitute for self. The gospel directs our attention to the being who raised Jesus from the dead, and who is to be identified with the one who brought Israel out of Egypt and who came in power upon the Church at Pentecost.

A distinctively Christian approach to personal growth arises from our response to this new centre of attention. It has been described in many ways but one of the most enduring is the notion of a pilgrimage. When we make the shift of focus called for by the gospel we embark on a voyage of discovery, an exploration, an exodus, a pilgrimage. And, perhaps, the pithiest summary of that pilgrimage is to be found in the words of Jesus: 'If any man would come after me, let him deny himself and take up his cross and follow me' (Mark 8:34).

Deny yourself

This is the essential preliminary step of the Christian pilgrimage. It entails the recognition that the quest for *self*-fulfilment is a dead end. The human potential movement may have produced many laudable results in terms of increased quality of life but as an overall vision for human life it is, in the end, futile. As Jesus adds to the words already quoted: 'whoever would save his life will lose it' (Mark 8:35a).

Denial of self may be the essential preliminary, but it is also the great stumbling block for many people. Many of its critics cannot see beyond this point; they take self-denial as all that Christianity has to say about personal growth. Unfortunately some Christian traditions have also made this mistake of believing that self-hatred was the proper Christian attitude to self. Not surprisingly, such Christianity is sometimes dismissed as encouraging an infantile dependence on God.

Take up your cross

Denial of self *is* only a preliminary stage. This should be clear to anyone who has ever tried it! If self-fulfilment is futile, so is the attempt to deny yourself. For self-denial on its own is every bit as self-centred as the quest for self-fulfilment. The one is merely the negative image of the other!

Thus Jesus points us to the next step: the cross. The cross of Jesus Christ is the fundamental discontinuity which lies between the two views of reality: the self-centred perspective and the God-centred.

What does he mean when he calls us to take up *our* cross? People often debase the idea by referring it to the greater or lesser troubles we all have to put up with in life: 'It's the cross I have to bear.' But the cross referred to by Jesus is his own. We are called to embrace the cross of Christ.

The point is that genuine personal growth is not to be achieved by our own efforts, either positive or negative. On the contrary, the way of the cross calls for the surrender of all our aspirations. We allow them to be put to death with Christ.

But the way of the cross extends beyond death. In embracing the cross of Christ we are also embracing Christ's redeeming work. Beyond the cross there is the promise of a new life: a life of participation in the life of Christ.

Many contemporary therapies, philosophies, and religious movements hold out the promise of personal transformation. The Christian way of the cross remains the most radical of all such promises.

Follow me

Christ calls us to follow him beyond the cross. But where? Unlike secular models of development, the gospel does not give us a detailed map of the journey. By thus refusing to generalise, every aspect of human experience can be incorporated into the experience of following Christ. There are as many paths as there are pilgrims following in the footsteps of Christ.

Nevertheless there are certain landmarks which distinguish certain journeys as Christian. As we have already noted, all such journeys begin at the cross.

Such journeys will increasingly be marked by the characteristics of Jesus' own life. They will become lives of sacrificial service.

They also have a distinctive goal. We do not follow Christ as isolated individuals. On the contrary, our spiritual journeys converge. We discover new personal relationships as we follow Christ: relationships made possible by the fact of our following him. Gradually we are incorporated into the body of Christ.

The ultimate end of this journey is mystical union with Christ. As individuals and as a community we are graciously permitted to share in the life of God. This is the divinisation of which the Eastern Orthodox Church speaks. We are divinised not deified: Christianity has never countenanced the notion, popular today, that we become God. What's the difference? It is analogous to the difference between an adopted heir and a natural heir: an adopted child is treated in all respects as a natural child, but it retains its own quite different genetic make-up. As adopted children of God, we are called to share in all the privileges and responsibilities of Christ.

What has this to do with personal development? In fact, the Bible does indicate a goal for personal development which parallels this gradual incorporation into the body of Christ. It speaks of us becoming mature in Christ. Such maturity entails personal transformation and genuine self-fulfilment. Indeed one of the most famous passages from Paul's letters exhorts us to 'be transformed by the renewal of your mind' (Rom. 12:2).

But the place of transformation has changed. For our secular society self-fulfilment is everything. For the Christian it is real but incidental. It is no more than a corollary of what really matters: love of God and of our fellow creatures.

THE SANCTIFIED TEMPERAMENT

Where does this discussion of Christian views of growth leave human psychology and, particularly, all that we have said about temperament?

As the rest of the book suggests, the weight of experience indicates that differences of temperament are not suppressed by the process of transformation that accompanies faith in Christ. Extraverts and introverts, intuitives, sensing types, thinkers and feelers all find a place in God's purposes.

This reflects the theological truth that the Church is called to embrace such differences without homogenising them. And this, in turn, is a reflection of God's own character.

Look at the world around you. Even where the town planners have done their worst, we cannot escape from the fact that we live in a world of the most amazing diversity. And all this is God's handiwork. God created all of this right down to the most trivial details. And yet none of those details is trivial to God. They all have a place in God's purposes.

Or consider the state to which we are called by Jesus Christ. We are called to be his friends not his slaves: to live in a personal relationship with God in Christ. Implicit in this call is a recognition of our integrity and individuality as creatures. The offer is not conditional on us becoming someone else.

Religious movements or spiritual disciplines which exclude such diversity are to that extent sub-Christian. Serried ranks of disciples all striving to be poor imitations of their leader's concept of a good disciple: this is the hallmark of the demonic rather than of the Holy Spirit.

Far from suppressing differences of temperament the Christian experience will actually enrich them. The extravert is called to express the Christian faith as an extravert, and the introvert as an introvert.

As we allow God to reshape our lives through the activity of the Holy Spirit we will find him complementing our natural strengths and compensating for our natural weaknesses. A glance at some of the New Testament lists of the gifts and fruit of the Holy Spirit makes very clear the extent to which the spiritual dimension can impinge upon the psychological. For many people this influence will be gradual, slowly transforming their lives as they live for Christ. For many others, it will mean a dramatic transformation. But in neither case does the Holy Spirit violate our integrity. The Holy Spirit may seek to transform us into more effective friends of God and servants of the world but he never seeks to possess us.

IN THE END . . .

The goal of the Christian journey is not self-fulfilment but incorporation into the body of Christ. At the same time it is an incorporation into the cosmic symphony of praise.

Hallesby concluded his study of temperament with the following words:

> our temperaments also will be perfected. On the new earth under the new heaven, the saved will reflect their Creator's

glory, not as exact copies of one another, but in an endless, varied multitude, proclaiming God's rich creation throughout eternity.

Then the divine masterpiece will be completed: The chorus of the redeemed of all ages will blend in perfect harmony to the praise of his glory.[3]

This does not mean an ultimate loss of identity. The symphony of praise is a harmony of all creatures not a unison note! Our different personalities, experiences, and temperaments all contribute something slightly different, something unique, to that harmony.

Appendix

What Is Lisa's Type?

Even from the brief description on p. 52 it is clear that she is an extravert. After all she is said to be talkative and gregarious.

Her friendliness, 'helpfulness', and love of popularity suggest that she is a feeling type.

The other preferences are not clear from the description. However, she does seem to relate to those around her through feeling. Since she is probably an extravert this suggests that she is a J rather than a P.

The choice of S or N is more speculative. She is described as trite and shallow. This may indicate a preference for S ('trite' and 'shallow' are the sort of epithets one might use in criticising an S). The fact that she finds it easy to achieve a rapport with others may also suggest a combination of sensing and feeling.

Thus Lisa is probably an ESFJ (or, less likely, an ENFJ).

Notes

CHAPTER 1: MANY MEMBERS, ONE BODY

1. O. Hallesby, *Temperament and the Christian Faith* (Minneapolis: Augsburg Publishing House, 1962), p. 7.
2. T. Roszak, *Person/Planet: The Creative Distintegration of Industrial Society* (London: Granada, 1981), p. 21.
3. For example, in their book *Personality Type and Religious Leadership* (Washington D.C.: Alban Institute, 1988), Roy Oswald and Otto Kroeger suggest that some temperaments are more inclined to sexual misconduct than others.
4. O. Hallesby, *op. cit.*, and Tim LaHaye, *Spirit Controlled Temperament* (Eastbourne: Kingsway, 1978).
5. O. Hallesby, *op. cit.*, p. 61.
6. D. R. Riso, *Personality Types: Using the Enneagram for Self-Discovery* (Wellingborough: Aquarian Press, 1988).
7. Carl Jung, *Man and His Symbols* (London: Aldus Books, 1964), pp. 60–1.
8. C. G. Jung, *Psychology and Religion: West and East*, Collected Works, vol. 11 (London: Routledge and Kegan Paul), p. 167.

CHAPTER 2: TALKING TEMPERAMENT: VOCABULARY

1. R. P. Feynman, *Surely You're Joking, Mr Feynman!* (London: Unwin Paperbacks), p. 105.
2. If this were a psychology textbook we would use the word psyche. However, we have opted for the more familiar 'soul'.
3. Adapted from G. Lawrence, *People Types and Tiger Stripes: A*

practical guide to learning styles (Gainsville, Florida: Center for the Application of Psychological Types), p. 22.

CHAPTER 3: TALKING TEMPERAMENT: GRAMMAR

1. The dominant function for each of the sixteen types is underlined.
2. I. Briggs Myers, *Gifts Differing* (Palo Alto, CA: Consulting Psychologists Press, 1980), p. 86.
3. C. G. Jung, *Psychological Types* in *The Portable Jung*, edited by Joseph Campbell (Penguin, 1976), p. 202.
4. *The Portable Jung*, edited by Joseph Campbell (Penguin, 1976), p. 209.
5. *ibid.*, p. 210.
6. Cited in I. Briggs Myers, *op. cit.*, p. 109.
7. I. Briggs Myers, *op. cit.*, p. 110.
8. *The Portable Jung*, p. 254.
9. I. Briggs Myers and M. H. McCaulley, *Manual: A Guide to the Development and Use of the Myers–Briggs Type Indicator* (Palo Alto: Consulting Psychologists Press, 1985), p. 27.
10. *The Portable Jung*, p. 260.
11. R. M. Oswald and O. Kroeger, *Personality Type and Religious Leadership* (Washington D.C.: Alban Institute, 1988), p. 85.
12. G. Lawrence, *People Types and Tiger Stripes: A practical guide to learning styles* (Gainsville, Florida: Center for Applications of Psychological Type, 1982), p. vii.
13. A brief explanation of Lisa's type is included in the Appendix, p. 130.

CHAPTER 4: PERSONALITIES IN PRAYER

1. D. Bloesch, *Essentials of Evangelical Theology, Vol. 2: Life, Ministry and Hope* (New York: Harper and Row, 1978), p. 59.
2. H. Nouwen, *Behold the Beauty of the Lord: Praying with Icons* (Notre Dame, Ind.: Ave Maria Press, 1987), p. 14.
3. T. E. Clarke, 'Jungian Types and Forms of Prayer', *Review for Religious*, Sept.–Oct. 1983, p. 667.

4. e.g., John Macquarrie, *Paths in Spirituality* (London: SCM, 1972), chapter 3.

5. Anthony de Mello, *Sadhana: A Way to God* (New York: Doubleday, 1984), p. 7.

6. Carolyn Osiek, 'The Spiritual Direction of "Thinking" Types', *Review for Religious*, March–April 1985, p. 212.

7. Augustine, *Confessions*, 7.10.

8. C. P. Michael and M. C. Norrissey, *Prayer and Temperament* (Charlottesville, VA: The Open Door, 1984).

9. Charles Keating, *Who We Are Is How We Pray: Matching Personality and Spirituality* (Mystic, CT: 23rd Publications, 1987), chapter 2.

10. Calvin, commenting on Gen. 2:15 in *Commentaries on the First Book of Moses, Vol. 1* (Edinburgh: Calvin Translation Society, 1848).

CHAPTER 5: COMMUNICATION AND THE GOOD NEWS

1. D. W. Hardy and D. F. Ford, *Jubilate: Theology in Praise* (London: DLT, 1984), p. 81.

2. Extract from *God's Cooperative Society* by Charles Marson quoted in Kenneth Leech, *Spirituality and Pastoral Care* (Sheldon Press, 1986), pp. 6–7.

3. K. Barth, *Church Dogmatics III/2* (T. and T. Clark, 1961), p. 161.

CHAPTER 6: PERSONALITY AND CHRISTIAN LEADERSHIP

1. David Watson, *I Believe in the Church* (Hodder and Stoughton, 1978), p. 246.

2. We use the Keirsey–Bates temperaments at this point because most of the published material on type and learning has been cast in this form.

Notes

CHAPTER 7: TRANSCENDING TEMPERAMENT

1. *The Portable Jung*, p. 7.
2. *ibid.*, p. 15.
3. O. Hallesby, *Temperament and the Christian Faith* (Minneapolis: Augsburg Publishing House, 1962), p. 106.

Useful Addresses

General Information about Myers–Briggs Type Indicator workshops may be obtained from:

BAPT (British Region: Association for Psychological Type), 7 Godfries Close, Tewin, Hertfordshire, AL6 OLQ (0992–501440)

A number of retreat houses and conference centres now offer Myers–Briggs workshops as part of their regular programme. Details of such workshops are often listed in *The Vision* (the journal of the National Retreat Association) which is available from bookshops or:

National Retreat Centre, Liddon House, 24 South Audley Street, London, W1Y 5DL (071–493–3534)